HOW to HAVE YOUR
SECOND CHILD FIRST

HOW to HAVE YOUR SECOND CHILD FIRST

100 Things That Are Good to Know ... the First Time Around

by Kerry Colburn & Rob Sorensen

CHRONICLE BOOKS

SAN FRANCISCO

*For our parents
and our daughters*

*Library of Congress
Cataloging-in-Publication
Data available.*

ISBN: 978-0-8118-6988-1

MANUFACTURED IN
Canada

DESIGNED BY
*Lesley Feldman
Feldmerica Industries*

10 9 8 7 6 5 4 3 2 1

Chronicle Books LLC
*680 Second Street
San Francisco, California 94107*

www.chroniclebooks.com

www.secondchildfirst.com

Having a baby changes everything. It opens the door to new emotions, priorities, challenges, successes—and utter mysteries. You enter a whole new life, after all, and it will likely feel completely foreign the first few months. After years of having a pretty good handle on how things work in the world, you might suddenly feel a bit lost, overwhelmed, or unsure of yourself as a brand-new parent. You will probably question every aspect of life with your new little person—*What should I buy for my baby? Who should come visit and when is a good time? When can I take a plane trip with my daughter? How long should I let my son cry? How will I know the right thing to do?*—and then second-guess each decision once you make it. And, unfortunately, you'll continually hear a wide range of contradictory advice, including from people whom you didn't even ask. When your stack of books, your mom, and even strangers on the elevator all have varying opinions on any given subject, who's got the right answer?

Relax. Any experienced parent will tell you that the first year is filled with discoveries, and included in those is figuring out what works for you and your baby. It's a constantly evolving, sometimes perplexing, and ultimately rewarding process. Along the way, try not to be so confounded by all the information (Do this! Don't do that! Don't *ever* do that!) that you can't see straight. Whether you believe it right now or not, you *will* come to trust yourself and your instincts. You *will* get to know your baby and yourself as a parent. Daily navigation of all the big and small parenting choices gets you up to speed in a hurry, and, eventually, all new parents must decide for themselves what feels right for their own family. But for now, what can really help is reassuring, empathetic, helpful advice from people who have been there. Twice.

Second-time parents—as savvy and unflappable as they seem when you see them at the park or the grocery store—

have all been sitting exactly where you are, not that long ago. They were hovering over their first babies and sweating about everything, and they clearly remember what it was like the (nerve-wracking) first time around. Now, these second-timers do things a little differently. And, by following their lead, so can you.

Case in Point:

FIRST-TIME PARENT: *Gotta get home to sterilize this dropped pacifier.*
SECOND-TIME PARENT: *Whoops, the baby's eating dirt again.*

FIRST-TIME PARENT: *The baby's sleeping, everybody be quiet.*
SECOND-TIME PARENT: *The baby's sleeping, let's have our friends over!*

FIRST-TIME PARENT: *Oh, let's see, I'd say it takes both of us about an hour to get our baby off to bed.*
SECOND-TIME PARENT: *Look, I can give my baby a sponge bath and read my toddler a bedtime story simultaneously!*

FIRST-TIME PARENT: *The baby's crying . . . we'd better leave.*
SECOND-TIME PARENT: *Crying? What crying?*

You see, once a second child comes along, not only are parents more confident from all that invaluable experience, they simply have less time, energy, and patience to spend doting, fussing, and perhaps even obsessing over every little thing. They know babies are resilient, that everything is a stage, and that things generally turn out okay. Add in the fact that they've given up on any illusions they might've had about how parenthood is "supposed" to be, and you get parents who approach every single task differently. You might say they lighten up. They definitely cut some corners. And, out of necessity, they become very, very efficient. They've learned that it's okay to do all sorts of things that they *never* would've considered the first time around.

Second-timers have no choice but to set aside some of the worry, find tricks to make things easier and faster, and factor in the needs of the whole family (yes, including themselves!) rather than just those of the baby. They've stopped sweating the small stuff, from funny noises in the night to traveling with baby to leaving their newborn with a sitter. No more compulsively looking things up in books, neurotically comparing notes with all the other parents, or feeling guilty over little mistakes made—no, second-time parents have learned to relax and enjoy more, stress less, and not hover.

Meanwhile, those wonderful second babies, with much less attention showered upon them, turn out just fine—and are often described as more adaptable, relaxed, and independent than their older siblings. Parents often wonder aloud at how "good" their second babies seem in comparison to how they remember their first—more patient, calmer, less work—but is it really the second child's disposition, or their own attitude, that has changed? Does number two really sleep better, or is it just that instead of being endlessly rocked and checked on, he's learned to soothe himself because Mom was busy giving the first child a bath?

Let's be honest. It isn't possible to *totally* embrace the more laid-back, everything's-okay attitude of a second-time parent the first time around. It's one thing to intellectually understand that the world doesn't end with a skipped nap, that a little crying never killed anyone, and that it really is okay to take a shower. But it's another thing to really feel it, believe it, and parent that way. Still, it helps to hear it straight from second-time parents that you *will* get through the seemingly endless ups and downs, that everything really *will* be fine.

And, as with any job, sometimes acting like you're more experienced than you actually are might make you start to feel more confident. We hope this book helps inspire that confidence. Rather than telling you all the things to worry about with your new baby and all the things not to do, this book is here to remind you of what second-time parents have learned you *can* do, what you *should* do. And really, you can do it.

We don't claim to be parenting experts, doctors, or psychologists. We are simply regular parents—well, the kind who had their first at an age north of thirty-five and who perhaps over-thought, over-researched, and over-fussed just a bit with that one. Today, with two kids ages four and two, we spend a lot of time talking to other second-time parents about all the things we do now that we never would've thought to do then, from changing a diaper in a restaurant booth to getting away overnight to letting our new baby sleep in a porta-crib in a corner of the home office without a mobile or "theme" wallpaper in sight. Rather than automatically thinking of all the things that could go wrong or all the things the other books advise against, we now look at life with children with the attitude "Well, what's the worst that can happen?"

This mental shift can give you all sorts of freedom. You see, sometimes, half the battle is just giving yourself permission to try something with your baby that may or may not work out, whether that's going out to dinner or trying to get a pedicure with her in tow. Second-time parents are much less worried about making a scene or causing their baby any inconvenience. They have relaxed their expectations on every front. They understand that life must go on, and baby is coming along for the ride.

We hope that by the time you finish our book, you'll approach every new baby challenge by asking yourself, *What would a second-time parent do?*

Here are one hundred things we wish we had known the first time around. We hope they help you—and help relax you—on your journey as a new parent.

{
AUTHORS' NOTE:
We are fortunate to have had complication-
free deliveries and two healthy children, which means we
are parenting and writing from this perspective. Special-needs
babies have, well, special needs, and therefore some of
the suggestions may not be practical or advisable for your family.
Your individual baby's health is of paramount importance.
Always consult your doctor with any questions.
}

YOU DON'T NEED
to BUY all THAT STUFF

One of the most overwhelming things facing first-time parents comes before baby is even born: sorting through all the information about what you need to buy for your little one. It's hard enough navigating the books, the doctor appointments, Mom's (and perhaps Dad's!) changing body, your emotions about becoming a parent— yet you're also pressured to decide between a Maclaren or a Bugaboo (or a college fund), a Boppy or a My Brest Friend, a station wagon or a minivan, high-end organic onesies or cheap packs from a discount store. . . . And why does everything have to have such confusing, non-sensical names to boot? (What is a Pack 'n Play anyway, and how does it differ from a Snap-N-Go?)

Take a deep breath and repeat after us: *I do not need it. I do not need it. I do not need it.*

Here's what you truly need for your child's first month of life:

- *An infant car seat*
- *A big package of newborn diapers*
- *A big package of unscented baby wipes (or cotton balls)*
- *A big package of onesies*
- *A place for the baby to sleep (might be a bassinet; Co-Sleeper; crib; your bed; or even a clean, dry sock drawer lined with safe padding)*

If you live in a colder climate, you can add a soft hat, a pair of socks, and a blanket to this list—but you'll get a million of these as gifts, and even your hospital will you send you home with them.

Consider absolutely everything else an extra. There is no need to buy any of it before the baby comes or even immediately thereafter. (Believe it or not, stores *will* continue to be open after the birth of your child.) It's actually prudent to wait to see how things go anyway—otherwise you might find yourself with ten sets of pajamas with feet only to discover that neither you nor your baby are fond of them, or a huge expensive jogging stroller that you wish you could trade in for a smaller, lighter version to maneuver more easily in and out of neighborhood stores. There's no way to know exactly what you will need (or how you'll want to use it) until baby appears and becomes part of your life. So keep it simple. Then order any additional items online, or borrow them, or send your spouse, mother, or friend out to pick up what you need—people want to help, and this gives them a task.

> *"Wipe warmers are a total scam.*
> *Think about it, what happens when you are out*
> *and about and need to change the baby—*
> *how are you going to warm the wipe? Better just*
> *get him used to room temperature."*
>
> —PAULA, MOM OF TWO, AGES 7 & 4

Now, every expectant mom (and maybe even some dads) has a mental list of everything she *has to buy* in order to sleep well at night, logic be damned. For one friend of ours, it was a gorgeous set of matching crib bedding; even though she knew her baby wouldn't be sleeping in the crib right away, it put her mind at ease to see everything set up beautifully while she was still pregnant. Another friend was obsessed with having enough socks and hats for her winter baby; meanwhile, her husband wanted to buy every childproofing item imaginable—even though it was only the second trimester. For you, it might be a bigger car, a fully decorated nursery, or drawers full of matching outfits. It's okay to succumb to your personal list. Think about what's weighing on your mind, and just buy it (and start a large envelope for baby-related receipts in case you need to return things). Then move on.

Good Baby Buys

You already know that beginning from day one, you will need only the things listed on page 12. But chances are you will still buy many more items early on. Use the following list as your guide when you go shopping or register for gifts. (Don't worry yet about gear you'll need months from now, like a high chair for when baby starts solids or a toddler car seat; you are always better off waiting to see what works for you when the time comes.)

▸ **PORTABLE CRIB.** Sometimes referred to by the brand name Pack 'n Play (by Graco), the generic name for this is a "play yard" (what our parents called a playpen). It's a handy portable crib that has a bassinet insert for newborns and can be collapsed to take to Grandma's. You can also use this at home in lieu of an expensive wooden crib. Baby can use it until past age two or whenever he's ready for a big bed.

▸ **BABY CARRIER.** A classic front carrier like the BabyBjörn (buy the one with lumbar support—it's worth the extra dough) is terrific; a carrier or wrap like the Ergo or the Moby offer other "wearing" positions. Most stores will let you try on a variety of baby carriers and can help you navigate them.

SNAP-N-GO. This frame turns your infant car seat into a stroller, thus rendering the purchase of a fancy stroller unnecessary for at least six to twelve months. Genius.

BABY MONITOR. Get the most basic model. You do *not* need one with a video screen or motion sensor. If you have a backyard, choose a monitor with a cordless feature.

VIBRATING INFANT SEAT. Otherwise known as a "bouncy seat," this cozy, portable contraption sits on the floor and is a handy place to transfer the baby to while in the kitchen or living room.

BATH-TIME GEAR. Infant tub, hooded towels, and small soft washcloths are nice to have, as are a pack of burp cloths (bar towels work great).

DIAPERING GEAR. A diaper-disposal system, a changing table (or something to use as one), and a pad with a washable cover make things easier.

DRUGSTORE ITEMS. Send your mom or a friend to pick these up as needed, or buy in advance if you like to feel *really* on the ball: baby nail clippers, cotton balls, infant pain medicine, natural baby wash, pacifiers (buy a couple of different styles), and diaper-rash cream or petroleum jelly.

Good Parent Buys

In your flurry of baby purchases, don't forget to buy things to make your life easier. Here's our totally subjective list of what we deem vital for new parents:

- **NURSING PILLOW (IF MOM PLANS TO NURSE).** Try the unfortunately named My Brest Friend for its flat, shelf-like surface for the baby.

- **THREE COMFY NURSING BRAS AND COTTON BREAST PADS.** You will need at least three bras, because one or two will constantly be in the wash. You will burn all of these when you're done breast-feeding, so don't go fancy.

- **COMFY CHAIR *WITH HEAD SUPPORT*.** Don't be fooled by that cool rocker or glider with the low back and modern lines—both parents must be able to easily lean the head back and doze. Trust us on this one.

- **EXERCISE BALL.** This is a cheap and easy alternative to your comfy chair. Many babies prefer a bouncing to a rocking motion, and the ball will save your legs and back like you wouldn't believe. It's great to have in a different room (or floor) than your comfy chair. Plus, it becomes a fitness tool for you—and a plaything for your child—later on!

TELEPHONE AND CELL PHONE HEADSETS. Because you will never have your hands free again.

INSULATED TRAVEL-STYLE MUG WITH NO-SPILL TOP. There is no reason for Mom or Dad to feel like they haven't had a cup of hot coffee in weeks. You will use this type of mug until your kids are in first grade, so buy the best.

EARPLUGS. See "Earplugs Are Your Friend" (pg. 118).

CABLE. You'll be watching a lot of TV at odd hours. Treat yourself to cable or a bunch of great TV series on DVD. It may also be time for TiVo or a DVR.

AUDIOBOOKS. Not a TV person? Download a bunch of great books (or check them out on CD) for times when you are trapped under your baby or endlessly walking with him.

MAGAZINES YOU CAN MANEUVER WITH ONE HAND. Give magazines a skim during constant newborn feedings or when baby is asleep on one arm.

MOM SNACKS. Mom will always be hungry. Give someone the task of mixing up a half dozen zip-top bags with almonds, dried cherries, dried apricots or mango, and chocolate chips; stash them in her purse, car, nightstand, diaper bag, nursing station, and stroller. Healthy energy bars, bananas, and bottles of water are also good to stock in these places.

[*No.*]
02

ASK FOR WHAT
you REALLY NEED

*For our first baby shower, we got lots of great stuff that we
needed—and more than our share of cute knitted hats, fancy
bibs, and adorable baby booties.* (Hint: babies don't need more than
one pair of booties, if any.) For our second pregnancy, we asked for
something different—we had a party where each guest brought a casserole, soup, or stew ready to freeze until the baby arrived. It was so wonderful to come home from the hospital and have ten ready-to-serve
meals waiting for us. So great, in fact, that we wish we would've known
to ask for that the first time.

Even if you want to have a traditional shower rather than a casserole party,
there are many other opportunities to have people help you with the
basics. When you are nearing the end of your pregnancy, and during
the first three months of your baby's life, all sorts of people will offer up
help. They'll ask what you need, what to bring, what they can do. This is
one time in your life *not* to be polite. Instead of saying, "Oh, nothing," give
'em a job. It makes people feel happy and useful to help out a new parent,
and it gives those lingering relatives or single friends something to do.

Contrary to what some first-timers believe, asking for help does not
make you seem incompetent—it actually makes you smart. So ask
your friend to pick up a package of diapers on her way over. Accept your
mother-in-law's offer to fold the laundry. Tell your office mates that what
you'd really love as a gift is a visit from a housecleaning service. See if
your neighbor can pick up coffee and a quart of milk on her way home
to save you a trip. Ask, ask, ask. People always say yes to new parents,
and chances are everyone will stop offering sooner than you think. And
do stand by this joking-but-not-really rule often enforced by experienced
parents: no one gets to come over and hold the baby without bringing a
meal for the whole family.

SECOND-TIMER TIP

If baby has one of those grandpas who likes to feel useful, schedule a weekend visit for him to install that shopping cart covers, drawer latches, doorknob covers, and other paraphernalia.

This rule applies out in the world as well. The second time around, we don't think twice about asking to borrow a diaper or other essential from any parent we see, asking friends to babysit when we need to escape, or requesting college-fund money rather than more unneeded toys as Christmas presents. We've also learned not to be shy about using our baby to get special treatment, and you shouldn't be either. Don't think of it as an admission of failure that you need to be treated differently. You *should* get special treatment, you deserve it! (Really, why aren't there specially designated parking spaces, grocery lines, and airport security lines for people with new babies?) Go ahead and request a better seat on the plane, call first dibs on the ladies room, or cut to the front of a long line when you're getting used to maneuvering through life with an infant. A sincere, *I'm sorry, would you mind terribly if I went first? My baby needs to [nurse, be changed, get to sleep, etc.]* goes a long way and can help you both get through your day more smoothly.

[No.] | YOUR BIRTH PLAN MIGHT
go **RIGHT** out the **WINDOW**

You can have a birth plan if you have specific desires about what you'd like to have happen in the delivery room. But no matter what you write down, discuss with your doctor, or envision in your head, something very different might transpire. Accept that. By the time you have your second child, you will understand that labor and delivery are full of surprises, not all of them pleasant, and the important thing is the health and safety of you and the baby—and nothing else. They don't have that birthing tub you requested? Room didn't look like the one on your tour? Forget about it. Once labor is under way, you will understand, with every fiber of your being, that none of it matters.

A friend recalls how angry she was about her emergency C-section after twelve hours of labor: "I was mad at the doctor because none of it was how I wanted it. My husband and I were so unprepared—we had brought a bottle of champagne to the hospital and thought it would be a piece of cake. It was not a piece of cake. The baby was small and my recovery was really tough." When it was time for her second child, she apologized to the doctor for her reaction. "It took a long time, but I had finally realized that the important thing was that my daughter got out safely. I thanked the doctor profusely for that because I didn't the first time."

You may have to deliver your baby with a doctor you've never met before. You may even end up in a hospital that you didn't expect. Labor might happen sooner or later than you prepared for, throwing all sorts of plans into havoc. It might happen so fast that your partner or midwife can't even get there, or so slow that you think you will never endure it. You may have to undergo a C-section even if you are opposed to it. You may want drugs and be refused them, or refuse them and have to take them. Even if it is smooth in every possible way, it's safe to assume it's nothing like you've seen in the movies.

So, how to prepare? Well, you really can't. Sure, you can watch the documentaries and take the classes. You can talk to other parents about their experiences. But if you are confident in the birthing team you have selected, and you've talked to them about any particular concerns or requests, your work is done for now. Most second-time parents agree that they wish they'd spent less time focusing on and reading about pregnancy and delivery, and more on life with a baby—which lasts a lot longer.

*"Be patient and enjoy every second
of your baby's first year."*

—ROSE, MOM OF TWO, AGES 14 & 12

[*No.*]
04

HOLD OFF
ON THOSE RSVPS

When you're pregnant for the first time, the idea of a foreign holiday, road trip, family reunion, or far-flung wedding soon after the baby arrives might not only sound doable, it might even sound fun. What a great opportunity to show off the newest member of the family!

But, even if childbirth goes as planned and you are blessed with a healthy, "easy" baby and a quick recovery, you may not feel up to it. The idea of packing, sleeping in a new place, and exposing your baby (and yourselves!) to all the stresses of travel just might not sit well with you. The truth is, you and your partner won't know how you're going to feel about making appearances at big events until *after* the big arrival.

If possible, hold off on those rock-solid RSVPs or nonrefundable plane tickets until after he's born. Tell hosts that you're a "maybe"—everyone will understand. In the end, if you have to miss out on something big this year, so be it—you don't need more pressure than you'll already have. If it's truly a can't-miss event, and you don't feel up to traveling with the baby, one of you can attend while the other stays home with baby and perhaps a grandparent or favorite aunt.

[No.] 05 YOU CAN TELL YOUR FAMILY
to **STAY AWAY** for a **WHILE**

Whether to include your family in the birth of your baby and her first few days of life is a very personal decision. Some people can't imagine having a baby without their mom, sister, or best friend close by, or even present in the delivery room. Other people's nesting instincts tell them to turn inward toward their new family unit, barring the door. What second-time parents have learned is this: you *do* have a choice.

"I didn't really think I had the option of telling my mom to not come right away," says a friend, whose baby represented the first grandchild on both sides. "But when the baby came early and my mom couldn't get there, I was happy having those first couple of days on our own. I have such fond memories of coming home from the hospital, just the three of us, and finding our own rhythm and routine. Now I advise my other friends to consider whether they might like a little time before the relatives descend."

Certainly, if you have a parent or close friend on whom you can lean emotionally and physically, and you like the idea of sharing the experience with that person, plan for it. There are lots of benefits to having another pair of hands those initial days—help with cooking, chores, and baby care. But if you are unsure, or have some family dynamics that make you feel stressed, it's okay to ask people—even your parents—to wait. If they don't have to book plane tickets, even better; tell them you'll decide when you're ready for visitors once you're home from the hospital. If they must purchase tickets in advance, ask them to come a week or two after your scheduled due date—you can always pay a change fee if you want them sooner. And truly, whether they appear on day one, five, or fifteen, your baby will still be brand-new, and the experience will still be magical for everyone.

Remember, this is the only time in your life when it will be just you and your baby. If you decide to have a second child, you will likely come home to a full house, including another adult in place from day one to help take care of your eldest—and any quiet one-on-one time with your new baby will be limited because you'll have to share your attentions. In other words, that beautiful bubble of sleeping together at odd hours, cuddling this new person endlessly, and focusing solely on one other being will be a thing of the past. So, do it the way *you* want the first time around. And whether or not your mom is in the next room, savor it.

[No.] 06 | THE BABY NAME YOU'VE CHOSEN is PERFECT

No matter whether you choose to name your baby after your great-aunt Margaret or make up a moniker like Zodon from your combined last names, someone will say something annoying. It will likely be one of the following:

- *What a coincidence! My daughter has three of those in her playgroup this year!*

- *Is that for a girl or a boy?*

- *Wow, that's not what we thought you'd pick.*

- *What are you going to call him for short?*

- *How brave of you to choose something so unusual [or old-fashioned].*

- *Oh, I could never use that name—that was my [evil ex-boyfriend, awful boss, first pet, high school nemesis]!*

Obviously, none of these comments is helpful, and who knows what possesses people to weigh in on something so personal to you. Second-time parents, who have been down this road before, are less likely to let it get under their skin. The bottom line is, don't let your family or friends sway you before you give birth (if you choose to tell them), and don't let strangers annoy you afterward. The name you have selected is just perfect.

[*No.*] 07 | AFTER DELIVERY, HAVE
EVERYTHING DELIVERED

You can have almost anything delivered to your doorstep these days. There's no better time than now to take advantage of this. Why lug a newborn to the grocery store during flu season (or in ninety-degree heat) if you don't have to? If you can, take the time to register with these kinds of services before the baby comes, or pass the task on to your spouse, mom, or close friend. It's ideal if you can even do "dry runs" to make sure you like what you've ordered so that you don't have to hassle with changing or canceling deliveries later. Here are some items to consider having appear on your doorstep.

▸ **DIAPERS.** Online retailers like Diapers.com and Amazon.com will deliver diapers, wipes, formula, and other baby needs, with free shipping if you meet their minimums (which is not hard to do).

▸ **GROCERIES.** Stores from supermarkets to Amazon.com deliver groceries now. Register for the basics you always need—milk, bread, bananas, eggs, yogurt, energy bars, paper towels, etc.—and you won't need to go to the store as often or make such big trips.

▸ **ORGANIC PRODUCE.** Many cities have organizations that deliver boxes of fresh produce to your door year-round. This is a great way to make sure you're eating right during this important nutritional time.

{ *Before the baby comes,*
make a point to pick up delivery and to-go
menus from every restaurant in your
neighborhood (or assign this task to a friend)
and put them in a handy accordion
file near the phone. }

▶ **DRUGSTORE AND BEAUTY PRODUCTS.** It may be some time before you feel like browsing the aisles of the beauty store for your favorite mascara or comparing prices on pain relievers. So order online now what you're running low on and you won't have to think about it later.

▶ **MAGAZINES.** You may not make your way through an entire book for a while. Take advantage of cheap subscription rates and order a magazine that will lift your spirits every time it hits the mailbox. Magazines might be just the thing to encourage you to put your feet up when you have a minute.

▶ **PREPARED FOOD.** Many cities have a variety of healthy prepared-meal services, separate from typical takeout, that allow you to choose from an extensive menu. Treating yourself to a dinner delivery even once a week might be a huge help to your family. Ask around, do an online search, or hint to friends that it would be a perfect gift.

[No.]
08 | YOU MAY THINK YOUR
BABY *is* FUNNY-LOOKING

Here's a secret: you may be taken aback when you study your baby for the first time, realizing that she doesn't look at all like you expected. And then you may feel terrible that you're a bit disappointed in her (quite possibly) peculiar appearance. How could you be so superficial?

We've been there. Our first was nearly ten pounds, with a dark faux-hawk hairstyle, puffy red face, enormous belly, fur on her bottom, and eyes that refused to open; she resembled an angry half animal–half Buddha more than anyone in our fair-haired, blue-eyed family. You may have heard that parents always find their own newborn to be unbelievably beautiful. Not true. Not all parents are blind to the baby acne, smashed nose, cradle cap, strangely shaped head, and overall oddball appearance of their new little person—especially since we all have a picture in our minds, one that's likely been influenced by all those four-month-olds being "born" on TV.

If you are less than enamored with your little one's appearance at first, don't worry. And don't feel badly. You will love her regardless—and thankfully she will soon blossom before your eyes.

[*No.*] 09 | THE FIRST FEW WEEKS
will **BLOW** *your* **MIND**

No matter how prepared you are, the time from your child's birth through his three-month birthday is really one of the toughest periods of your life—and the most amazing. You will even hear this period dubbed "the fourth trimester," because it really feels like an extension of pregnancy, whereby the baby depends on you so completely, and yet he really doesn't give you anything in return. The basic things you expect from a new baby, and have been waiting all this time for—the smile, the adoring gaze, the mere recognition of you as his life-giving parent—are simply not there yet. When this new baby is demanding so much from you, it can be brutal to be rewarded with nothing but a seemingly endless blur of soiled diapers, hungry cries in the night, and mysterious needs that somehow can't be met no matter how hard you try.

You likely will have never experienced such highs and such lows. Elation and despair will both take up residence in your house, and you'll never know which one is going to hit you between the eyes. You will be sleep deprived, worried, hormonal, hungry, fed up, in awe. You will wonder how this completely alien being ended up with you, and what you're supposed to do with him now. You will not know where the days go, but they will go—usually either way too quickly or way too slowly. You will weep and you will (hopefully) laugh, and you will be both stunned at what you can do and panicked that you have no idea what you're doing.

Many experienced parents agree that those first twelve weeks are just as overwhelming and topsy-turvy the second, third, and fourth times around—which means there is simply no way to prepare your way out of them. You can read all the books, take the prep classes, outfit your home with every possible convenience, and *still*. Still you come home with an infant you've never seen before who relies on you for every possible element of his survival. The relentlessness of parenthood will come at you like a hurricane, and you will begin to understand that this is forever. You might think, *How can I possibly do this job? And why on Earth did I sign up for it?* When these questions really start to freak you out, remember what all experienced parents know that you may not yet: to panic is normal. While it may be hard to believe, this phase *will* pass.

"Those first three months are the endurance test," says a dad of three. "We've learned to just clear the decks. We stock the freezer and the pantry, we line up childcare help, we make sure we have as few commitments as possible at work and at home. Basically, we prep the nest as best we can. That's all you can do. Then we expect to just put those blinders on and soldier through it."

And rest assured, blazing moments of love and pride and joy will repeatedly pierce through the fog of those first three months. Somehow, in the midst of changing another diaper and preparing another bottle and waking up in the middle of the night yet again, you will feel immense pride for creating this new life and guiding him through each moment. Each day, he gets stronger and more fascinating. Each day, he feels more like yours, like you belong together. Each day, you are closer to that three-month mark, when new parents high-five each other and realize it only gets better and more fun from here. In the end, the newborn weeks comprise such an unbelievably short period of time. You will have good moments and bad, but you will get through it—and when you do, you will have reached the first big milestone of parenthood. You will have completed the fourth and final trimester. Congratulations!

[No.] 10   TAKE ADVANTAGE OF HOW MUCH *your* NEWBORN SLEEPS

During the first three months, newborns sleep as much as sixteen hours per day. So why are you always tired? Besides the fact that you're in recovery (and possibly also in shock) from the birth, it's because those hours are not consecutive—not by a long shot. Still, that's a lot of time, albeit fragmented. So although your baby may look small and fragile, this is actually the easiest time to travel and go to restaurants, as well as to allow yourself to nap and recover.

> *"Travel as much as you can when your baby is young. There is no better travel companion than someone who sleeps most of the way there, fits in your lap, and doesn't require his own full-price ticket."*
>
> —JENNIFER, MOM OF TWO, AGES 3 & 2

Don't be scared to try a trip, a party, a leisurely meal at a favorite eatery, or even an afternoon movie during your baby's first weeks. You will see second-timers doing it all the time. Chances are, she will sleep through at least a good portion of it—and you'll feel both revived and proud for making the attempt.

SECOND-TIMER TIP

Don't rush in to get your baby out of the crib at her first peep. If given a chance, she may be the one who wakes up slowly and chatters contentedly to herself—allowing you a few extra minutes each morning.

"We went to Hawaii four weeks after our second child was born," an experienced dad says. "That's where we spent my wife's maternity leave. It was great—while the baby was dozing in her car seat, the rest of us enjoyed the beach, barbecues, the beautiful warm weather. We would never—never!—have been brave enough to do it with the first baby. But it was the perfect thing to do with our second."

[No.] 11

DON'T FEAR THE
NIGHTTIME NOISES

New babies are the noisiest sleepers you can imagine. They snort, snuffle, whine, and gurgle like angry little warthogs. You might be awakened many times in the night, stunned that something that weighs only a few pounds can make such a ruckus and certain that he must "need" something. The thing is, if it's not feeding time, he's just a noisy newborn finding his way.

One thing the books don't necessarily tell you is that it's perfectly normal for new babies (and, some say, particularly C-section babies) to make all sorts of wet grunting sounds during their first weeks while their sinuses are still developing. Also, new babies have somewhat irregular respiratory patterns; yours may seem to repeatedly stop breathing for a few seconds before normal breathing resumes—totally anxiety-producing if you're not accustomed to it. If your baby's color is normal while he's sleeping, then most likely he's just fine. Of course, call your doctor immediately if your baby's color looks unusual, or if he seems really uncomfortable or short of breath while making these noises. But as long as he's sleeping through the commotion, you should too.

See also, "Your Baby Will Be Just Fine in His Own Room" (pg. 85) and "Earplugs Are Your Friend" (pg. 118).

[No.] 12 | BREAST-FEEDING
MIGHT NOT COME EASY

Unlike many aspects of baby care, there's simply no way to practice breast-feeding ahead of time. No matter how many nieces and nephews you've rocked to sleep, or how much babysitting experience you've clocked over the years, this is one thing you've never done. This strikes real fear in some first-time parents, especially those who have heard nerve-wracking nursing tales with terms like "engorgement," "pumping," "clogged ducts," and "bad latches"—all of which can sound like a particularly grueling episode of a home rennovation show. Other first-timers might feel positively laissez-faire about this new endeavor: after all, the baby arrives and you put it on a breast and that's that, right?

{

SECOND-TIMER TIP

If your nipples are particularly sore from rough, early sessions of breast-feeding, ask the hospital nurse for nipple shields— flexible plastic nipple covers with holes that baby can nurse through. They are also available at birthing/baby-supply stores.

}

Hopefully, but not always. The truth is, some babies take to it easier than others. Sometimes health issues or premature delivery complicate the process; other times, your baby is dubbed a "sluggish" or an "aggressive" sucker, each of which comes with its own challenges. And barring any issues whatsoever, you both just need some practice to get it right. A class or instructional video before delivery can be helpful. Even more helpful are those angels known as labor and delivery nurses, or on-site lactation consultants, whom the hospital has on staff. Throw all modesty out the window (if you haven't already) and let them manipulate your bare breast and the baby's mouth to get the proper alignment. Ask for tips on everything from what level to adjust your bed to what holds you might try to what will soothe sore nipples. Buzz them repeatedly until you find the person who helps you the most. And remember, one of the cruel jokes of motherhood is that your baby is born hungry and milk doesn't come in right away, so the hospital stay is often the hardest part of the nursing phase. It usually gets easier once everything is flowing, commonly a day or two after you get home.

Second-time moms tend to have an easier time with breast-feeding if they were successful with it before, as milk tends to come in quicker, and they've learned from previous painful mistakes, like letting a new baby nurse for way too long the first few sessions before nipples have "toughened up." They've also learned some tricks of the trade:

▶ **USE A PILLOW.** A nursing pillow or large, firm cushion is invaluable in keeping the baby at the right level for nursing without killing your arms and neck.

▶ **USE THE RIGHT CHAIR.** Various leg and back ailments can arise from contorting your body while nursing. Do your best to keep both feet on the floor, even if it means investing in a low stepstool or an angled nursing stool. When possible, use a comfy chair with good back support and armrests.

SECOND-TIMER TIP

*You can buy or rent a pump, but,
ideally, borrow one from a friend or family
member (just sterilize the components
and hoses or buy those new)—you may not end
up using it much, and all moms want to
get rid of it when they're done.*

▶ **KEEP YOUR HEAD UP.** Tempting as it is to gaze at your baby, you can really hurt your neck after a while. Remember to look out at the horizon (or the TV) as often as you can.

▶ **HAVE LANOLIN ON HAND.** Dry, cracked nipples require Lansinoh, the only cream you should put on your nipples—and it doesn't need to be wiped off before baby latches on again. Keep small tubes of it in your nursing pillow's pocket and anywhere else you nurse, until you find you have achieved "toughened nipples."

▶ **BUY BURN PADS.** In the hospital, you may be offered weird blue gel pads to put on your breasts. These are lifesavers for sore, cracked nipples and are available at drugstores, usually in the burn-relief area and sometimes under the brand name Soothies.

▶ **BUY BREAST PADS.** Washable cotton breast pads are going to be part of your life for a long time. Buy a bunch and you won't have to worry about leakage; throw them in the wash with your bras.

▶ **FROZEN PEAS ARE NOT JUST FOR DINNER.** When breasts are engorged or sore, shove a bag of frozen peas into your nursing bra.

▶ **WHEN IN DOUBT, CALL A PROFESSIONAL.** Most hospitals offer a new-mom advice line staffed with postnatal nurses. They can also refer you to a lactation consultant who makes house calls if you're having a hard time. These women are amazing. Don't hesitate to use them if you need help.

Here's what you learn with experience: breast-feeding may come easily to you, or it may be harder than you think. You may find it to be one of the most rewarding and magical aspects of new parenthood, or you might not. You may think you're going to do it for a year and only last a few weeks, or you may expect to do it for a few weeks and keep at it until toddlerhood or beyond. Like we said, there's no way to truly prepare for this one and know how it's going to be until you're in the middle of it. The important thing to remember is that if breast-feeding is important to you, and you are willing to ask for help if you encounter obstacles, you will likely find your way past the bumps. And if it doesn't work for you and your baby, you have perfectly healthy alternatives.

See also, "Formula Is Totally Fine," next.

FORMULA IS
TOTALLY FINE

These days, as opposed to thirty years ago, new moms feel a lot of pressure to breast-feed at all costs, and we know some who feel ostracized by other moms when they don't. We have all heard the arguments for why "breast is best," but if you decide nursing is not for you—*for whatever reason*—rest assured that formula is a terrific alternative.

> *"I just said no to pumping after my first. I never liked it and was never good at it. When it was time to introduce the bottle to my youngest, I used formula for that and breast-fed the rest of the time. It worked great for me."*
>
> —JANE, MOM OF THREE, AGES 10, 6 & 1

Many people sail through breast-feeding just fine, and if this is your choice, hopefully that will be the case for you. But despite your best intentions, you may encounter problems. You may not like it. Your baby might not take to it. You may have to follow some sort of convoluted feeding and pumping routine to make supply match demand. You may find it too taxing and begin to feel resentful, alienated, and angry. You may have trouble balancing it with a return to work. If so, you may come to ask yourself whether the stress is outweighing the benefits. Only you will be able to decide this. Unfortunately, besides your own emotions about stopping (or not starting) breast-feeding, there is the outside pressure. Try not to let it sway you. Read the research or talk to your doctor about formula, and you will realize your baby will be just fine nutritionally. Or ask any second-time moms (who tend to shorten the length of time spent breast-feeding with the subsequent child) and chances are, they will point out that a stressed-out, unhappy mom is not doing herself or her child any favors.

"I finally asked myself what my goal was," says one mom who endured pumping, nursing, and using a feeding tube around the clock for her sluggish eater. "Is my goal to breast-feed exclusively no matter what, or is my goal simply to feed my baby well and have us be happy and healthy? I decided it was the latter and that I could achieve that—by using formula."

> *"If you're supplementing with formula,*
> *keep baby bottles with premeasured dry*
> *formula in them next to your bed, plus bottles*
> *of water. You can quickly mix a bottle*
> *in the middle of the night—no need to fumble*
> *your way to the kitchen."*
>
> **—REGAN, MOM OF TWO, AGES 4 & 2**

Even if you don't use formula all the time, you can work it into your nursing schedule to make life easier. When your pediatrician asks you to introduce the bottle, for example, you can try formula for those isolated feedings and save yourself from having to pump breast milk. Or you can breast-feed all day, but let your partner give a bottle of formula in the middle of the night so you can rest, provided your full breasts will let you. Will your baby refuse it? Will your breasts leak by morning? You never know until you try. Second-time parents have learned to ask themselves what's best for everyone in the family—and if some combination of formula and nursing works well and saves mom some time, that's great.

"I just wasn't comfortable nursing at my older child's sports games, birthday parties, and playdates," says one second-time mom. "I didn't think twice about using formula for those feedings, because pumping was hard for me and I never had time for it."

The bottom line is that there's no need to kill yourself to breast-feed, or to give yourself undue pressure to continue it longer than is working for you. Yes, breast-feeding is considered nutritionally best. It is also cheaper and doesn't require a lot of equipment. But it does take a *lot* of time. Our generation is lucky to have excellent alternatives, including state-of-the-art and even organic formula options. It may be hard for your spouse, family and friends, or other new moms to understand the emotions tied up in the decisions surrounding your feeding choices, but, in the end, you have to do what you feel is best. Rest assured that formula is a totally wonderful alternative for your baby. Love is infinitely more important.

"My first child was born early
and small. Per doctor's orders, I had to
feed him every three hours around
the clock for three months. Needless to say,
I never slept more than two hours during
those early months. With my second child, I
learned that if my husband could give
the baby formula in the night so I could sleep,
I'd be a better mom during the day."

—ANGI, MOM OF TWO, AGES 7 & 5

FIND A SUPPORT
SYSTEM—EARLY

There's nothing wrong with needing a support system—in fact, parenting would likely be a much healthier experience if everyone had one in place from pregnancy on. It's important to find your "village" that will help you to raise your child, whether it's an organization, trusted friends or neighbors, or family members who live nearby. If you reside in a midsize or large city, you'll have access to everything from new-parents' groups that match you by your child's birth date and neighborhood (ask at your birthing facility and register before baby comes) to new-parent classes to informal family social clubs that meet at your local community center or library. Beyond this, your pediatrician can direct you to parenting coaches, support groups, and family therapists.

If you don't know your neighbors well already, the birth of your baby is a great excuse to become friendly, especially with those who have small children of their own. You might start a babysitting swap, trading one morning or evening per week to give the parents some free time, or just have each other's numbers on hand to call if you need a half-hour break or some solid advice. Plus, the better you get to know them now, the more fun future playdates may be!

Nowadays, many new parents live far from their own families, and, in some cases, the baby's grandparents might be too elderly to provide much relief. Even if you don't consider yourself a "joiner" and are resistant to signing up for a group, think of it this way: if you go to a couple of parents' club meetings and come away with just one other couple you can imagine spending more time with (and whom you can call in a pinch), it's been worth it.

CHANGING TABLES
are NOT IMPERATIVE

With our first child, we ran up a significant flight of stairs for every single diaper change. This fact now boggles our minds. Now, with two children, we don't have the time or energy to go up the stairs any more than we have to . . . not to mention the fact that we have a preschooler who could get into all sorts of mischief during the two unsupervised minutes it takes to go between floors. With our firstborn, we considered buying a second changing table for the ground floor. Were we crazy? Now we have a bath towel on the dining room table (and have had it there for a solid year)—voilà! Changing table! And it's just the right height. Who sits down for dinner anymore anyway? Yes, you have to hold on to your child when you don't have that dinky little strap that comes with the changing table. (*Always* keep a hand on a baby who's on an elevated surface.) It's a small price to pay.

SECOND-TIMER TIP

If your older baby tends to furiously twist and roll during diaper changes, try handing her something that is safe but not a toy—a sealed spice jar she can shake, a roll of masking tape, your cell phone, or keys. Sometimes it's the new, non-baby things that distract her long enough to do the job.

Second-time parents recommend a variety of other spaces: a large ottoman, the guest bed, the coffee table, the top of the toy box, and, of course, the largest changing table in the house—the floor.

This theory holds when you leave the house too. No changing table at the restaurant, store, or coffee shop you find yourself in? Shame on them—and be sure you put a note in the comment box or make your feelings known to the manager. But don't scurry home. Unless you've got some unholy mess to deal with and would be more comfortable leaving, throw down a blanket and change your baby on the booth, couch, table, or floor. The backseat or interior hatchback of your car also makes a handy changing table in a pinch. This will seem much more natural if you've become used to commando diaper changes in different places at home.

"Wipes are great for when you need them, but you don't have to use them for every diaper change when the baby's only gone number one—especially when you're in a difficult spot or when baby gets older and diaper changing becomes a wrestling match. Pee is sterile, right? Sometimes you just gotta skip the wipe and go right for the dipe!"

—ELIZA, MOM OF TWO, AGES 4 & 3

[*No.*]
16

THERE'S NO NEED TO
TIPTOE *around* YOUR BABY

"My house is so noisy all the time!" says a friend and parent of three. "It drives me crazy, but the baby sleeps right through it."

For the first few months of our first baby's life, we had a large "Do not ring!" sign plastered over the front doorbell. At her bedtime, guests went home, the upstairs phone ringer was turned off, and no major appliances were turned on until morning. My, how things have changed.

Our second child sleeps in our home office, right behind the big-screen TV. We not only run the washing machine, watch movies, and vacuum while she sleeps, we often have friends over for movie night or cocktails. She has learned to tolerate not only doorbells, but the laughter, wails, and tantrums of a loud four-year-old. And we have learned that there is a big upside to this: the girl can sleep anywhere, on a noisy car ride, in a new house with new noises, or in our living room while our oldest dances to music. Second children simply don't get the luxury of silent houses. (Believe me, our house is never silent.)

> *"Don't struggle with your baby to perform grooming tasks. Trim his nails or his bangs while he's asleep—in the car seat worked best for me."*
>
> **—ERIN, MOM OF TWO, AGES 8 & 4**

Here's the thing: as you've probably read, the womb is an incredibly noisy place. Noise is fine with babies, and familiar. If you condition him to sleep only in utter quiet, that is likely what will be necessary to get him to nod off in the future. That's going to make things hard for both of you. If, on the other hand, you teach him to find solace with the ambient noise of an active household, your baby will be more adaptable—and you get more freedom. So go about your business during the day, and, while you're at it, call your friends and tell them to come over for drinks at eight. Shake those martinis, turn on some lounge music, and toast to what second-time parents call the new happy hour—the one that starts immediately after bedtime.

[No.] 17 | YOU REALLY CAN
TAKE a SHOWER

It may be the most universal complaint of any new mom: "I can't even seem to take a shower!" Many resort to showering late at night out of desperation, likely feeling resentful and wishing they were already in bed. Second-time parents know that happy parents make happy babies, and if Mama would be happier with a shower (and child number one is at school, watching a DVD you swore you'd never resort to, or otherwise occupied for the moment), then Mama is going to take a shower. So what to do to make it as pleasant as possible for both of you? The main obstacle with newborns is where to physically put the baby, if leaving her in the crib or bassinet is not working or you're simply too worried to have her in the next room during those first few weeks. Try the following ideas, along with talking or singing to your baby (or listening to a favorite CD) while you lather up. If you don't have a glass shower door, leave the shower curtain open and play peekaboo.

Try putting your new baby in:

▸ A Moses basket, either on the floor or inside the bathtub, if separate from the shower

▸ A vibrating infant seat or swing with a toy bar

▸ The infant car seat

When they get a little older (four to seven months), you have more options. Try a Jolly Jumper or an Exersaucer, if you can wedge one into your bathroom. At six months and older, when baby can confidently sit up, place her baby tub seat (the ring kind with the suction cups) at the far end of the shower with a few bath toys within reach. Before you bring your baby into the mix, test out the angle of the spray; adjust the shower-head to allow her to see the water, and perhaps feel it on her toes, without surprising her with a full soak. Then do a dry run—get her used to the location before you turn on the water by singing and playing while you're seated next to her. Seem okay? Then turn on the shower gently, testing for temperature. Show your baby through your voice and manner that this is a fun activity, not something you must rush through or worry about. Congratulations! You have begun an efficient ritual of showering together that may continue well into preschool. This option is especially useful if you have a handheld shower nozzle; wash yourself and then give baby a gentle rinse, and you can cross baby's bath off your list.

The key here, as with most experiments with babies, is not to give up after one or two scream-fests. (Second-time parents don't acquiesce to their babies so easily; you will rarely hear them say things like, "My baby just doesn't like the stroller" or "My baby only eats homemade baby food"—they will just keep plugging away until the little one gets used to it.) Like any regular occurrence in your house, your baby will likely take to shower time if it becomes a familiar and happy routine, so your stress won't help. Instead, show her through your actions how fun it's going to be—and believe it. Sell it! "Hooray, lucky baby, it's shower time!" Try a few different approaches until you find one that works. For example, infant car seat + mirror toy + pacifier + a favorite song, especially right after a feeding, might be a winning combination that allows you a luxurious shower with no tears (for either of you). And remember, likes and dislikes change rapidly during the first year—if one method is no longer working, try another, even if she balked at it last time. Who knows, in the end she might come to truly love the ten minutes when she smells your coconut shampoo and hears the enjoyable sound of water running while you sing her favorite song.

Now, keep in mind that you don't *have* to do any of this. At any age, you can indeed put your baby safely in her crib or play yard and take a quick shower. If it's necessary for your mental health, self-image, or plans for the day, just do it—and quickly come back for a cuddle in your bathrobe, warm and clean. It's part of her ongoing process of learning that you do leave sometimes, but you always come back.

NURSING DOESN'T HAVE TO COMPLETELY TAKE OVER *your* LIFE

If you're breast-feeding, there's no way around having it on the brain, since you're likely nursing every couple of hours at first. It might seem like every time you finish, it's time to start again, and you're probably wondering, *How will I ever leave the house?* Before going anywhere, you have to stop and think, *How long will this take? Where will I nurse? What should I wear?*

But second-time moms can't let the inconveniences of nursing rule the day, and therefore they just make it work. (Of course, this gets more feasible once you get through the first couple of months and demand settles down a tiny bit.) A lot depends on your comfort level with breast-feeding in strange places—the car or a restaurant, for example—versus always being home in your perfect chair. Another consideration is whether you're willing to pump and store milk and/or occasionally substitute formula into your round-the-clock breast-feeding regimen.

If you're shy about nursing in public, you may want to invest in a couple of nursing tops, which have discreet openings for easy access to your nipples so you don't have to hike up your whole shirt. (Nursing tops can be expensive. Make your own by cutting a hole for each breast out of an old T-shirt and wear this under another top. When you hike up your outer top, the T-shirt will still cover your belly.) You might also want to keep a couple of small blankets or custom nursing bibs in your car or diaper bag. Also, don't be shy about asking any restaurant, store, or shopping center about a good ladies' lounge or nursing spot. Your car can be a great backup—you have climate control, the radio, and your cell phone to keep you company; a modicum of privacy; and the door handle, which is often at the perfect height to rest your elbow on.

If you truly find that you'd rather be at home to nurse, you're not alone. Just take solace in the fact that the nursing sessions will get farther and farther apart over time, and you'll soon actually be able to leave for the entire afternoon!

See also, "You Can Leave Your Baby with Other People" (pg. 98) and "Formula Is Totally Fine" (pg. 34).

[No.] 19

YOU DON'T HAVE TO CHANGE YOUR NEWBORN'S

DIAPER at NIGHT

 *We remember automatically changing our firstborn's diaper when she woke for middle-of-the-night feedings.* We just thought that was what you were supposed to do—keep her dry, all night long. The truth is, with today's superdiapers, it's usually not necessary—and it only wakes the baby (and you) more than is needed for a feeding. Instead, use the trusted second-time parent "sniff test"—if you pick him up out of his crib and can't easily smell poop, don't even check his diaper. (At the next wake-up call, if there is one, you can add in a quick squeeze of his diaper to see if it's really full or has leaked, and do a change if needed.)

> *"I didn't want my baby to be the slightest bit uncomfortable, so I changed his diaper at almost every feeding. As an exhausted new mom, even this small effort seemed monumental. When my daughter was born two years later, we simply put her in a diaper that was one size bigger at night so it could hold more. I didn't bother changing her diaper at all during the night unless it was especially aromatic. We both got back to sleep much faster."*
>
> **—ANNE, MOM OF TWO, AGES 4 & 2**

WASH ALL THE FAMILY

LAUNDRY TOGETHER

Do you think any second-time parent gives a moment's thought to separating the new baby's laundry from the rest of the family's—much less buying a separate detergent for that purpose? No way. By the time you have number two, that concept has gone the way of separating lights from darks—these days, we're just thankful if all of it gets shoved in the machine at some point. At any rate, it's not necessary that baby gets her own load. Unless your baby has some sort of medically documented skin condition and your pediatrician recommends a few weeks of a special baby detergent like Dreft, don't generate any unnecessary work for yourself. (And, by the way, if she hasn't peed through her pj's, there is really no reason not to leave your baby in them all day.)

> *"With my first daughter, every single clothing and bedding item got washed in gentler detergent; even my mom insisted on it. Well, by number two, everything got dumped in with the Tide, and, lo and behold, she didn't break out in a funky rash, get deathly ill, or even notice the difference."*
>
> —PAULA, MOM OF TWO, AGES 8 & 6

YOU DON'T HAVE TO STERILIZE

EVERY LITTLE THING

Second children grow up in a house that is full of their big brother or sister's toys, books, dishes . . . and germs. Not only is there no time to obsess about sterilizing, there is simply the realization that when a baby lives with a toddler or preschooler who is out in the world—including on playdates, at the library, and at daycare or preschool—there is no chance of that perfect, sterile bubble around baby that might've been the goal the first time around. Sure, sterilize your infant's bottles, nipples, and pacifiers the first time you use them. (You don't need to buy any fancy sterilizing bags or other contraptions; just throw everything into a pot of boiling water on the stove for five minutes.) But when he begins crawling, he begins exploring—mostly with his mouth—and second-timers know that you simply can't expect everything he licks to be clean.

"Once babies start putting things in their mouths, there is no point in sterilizing—a relatively clean toy in your house will have more germs on it than any soother or bottle," says a mom of three. "At this point, I just wash bottles and soothers with hot soapy water for daily use and put them through the dishwasher on the 'sani-rinse' cycle once a week." Also wash favorite "mouth toys" like hard plastic dolls, blocks, and tub toys every couple of weeks. But sterilizing all that stuff? Don't bother!

[No.] 22 | DON'T DWELL ON THINGS you CAN'T CONTROL

Parenthood opens the door to a world of anxiety-producing what-ifs. Every new parent checks to make sure the baby is still breathing. Every new parent worries about scary things like SIDS. Every new parent sees his or her baby enter the world and becomes painfully aware of all its possible dangers. When it comes to our own lives, we've adapted to this; after all, our survival depends on not staying in the house every day, worrying about what could befall us on our way to work. But a baby comes along and everything feels different. There's another entity to worry about, a helpless one at that, one you are utterly responsible for. Likely, you began this cycle of parental worry during pregnancy, reading statistics and stressing over risk test results, asking again and again, What if . . . ?

Second-time parents aren't immune from this constant concern for their children—far from it. But they have lived through the first scares and surprises, be they a scraped knee, an unexpected allergy, or something more serious, and they kept going. One thing parenthood teaches you, on a whole new level, is that life is a beautiful and fragile thing. To the best of your ability, be diligent when it comes to your child's health and safety. Be as protective as is prudent. Parent well and confidently. But don't teach your child to live in fear of what might happen. Strive to release yourself from constant worry about things you can't predict or control.

[No.] 23 — USE ANY MEANS NECESSARY TO GET *through* ROUGH PATCHES

One set of new parents admitted that they had finally gotten their baby to sleep through the night by keeping her tightly swaddled in a mechanical swing, which they kept running all night. Another couple let their baby sleep in his infant car seat instead of his expensive crib, because otherwise he kept flipping over in the night and waking himself up. Other parents expressed worry about using the swaddle blankets with the ties to soothe their baby: "It kind of seems like a Houdini trap," the new dad admits. "But it works, so we can't stop using it." Others confessed to parking the baby in front of a running dishwasher (even when it was empty) or sitting with her for long stretches on top of a spinning washing machine, because those were the moments she never cried.

Parents do a lot of funny things to get their children to sleep or to just stop crying: long drives in the car, even in the middle of the night; experiments with swings, slings, and bouncers; ridiculously long walks with various baby carriers or strollers; white noise; frozen waffles and spoons to chew on for a few minutes of quiet. You name it, a new parent has tried it. And here are three words you'll hear over and over from second-time parents: *hey, whatever works*. There is no need to feel inadequate because you can't soothe your baby simply by rocking her in your arms. There is no need to hide the fact you've got some crazy routine going that occasionally works when nothing else does. Sometimes, you've got to rely on outside gadgets or tricks to get through the rough patches—and second-timers don't think twice about it.

> *"Don't get too caught up during each difficult phase of a baby's development. I now realize these challenging phases pass so quickly that, by the time you have come up with a solution, you are on to the next event."*
>
> —JANE, MOM OF THREE, AGES 10, 6 & 1

If you're concerned that you may actually be doing something detrimental, speak to your pediatrician or the on-call nurse to double-check. In the end, your doctor is the only outside opinion that matters—so forget about what your mother-in-law thinks. If your baby will only give you some peace today while strapped in the vibrating seat with the shower running and Mozart on a boom box, go ahead and do it—after all, next week you'll probably have to figure out something else.

PUT "ME TIME" INTO
MATERNITY LEAVE

If you are lucky enough to have a nice long maternity or paternity leave, you might find that after the first few weeks you begin to feel frustrated, antsy, trapped, or lonely. You may begin to crave some adult interaction, more structure to your day, and a sense of accomplishing tasks other than getting the laundry done. That's when you know it's time to start venturing out into the world a little more, doing things that you enjoyed before the baby was born. Of course, parents of two or more children get accustomed to bringing the baby along to the children's museum, library, park, and various other locales with older siblings. Might as well get some practice now by scheduling some parent playdates!

Meeting friends for coffee is a great way to start socializing again, especially since lots of babies nap in the late morning. Choose an ideal time, but even if things go off-schedule with your baby that day (as they probably will), coffee dates are generally easy to move around. Work up to meeting friends, former coworkers, or your partner for lunch.

Shopping is another great activity with an infant—if awake, he has lots to look at, and many department stores and children's stores have nice lounges with changing tables and usually a comfy place to feed your baby. Don't forget to buy a few pretty things for yourself along the way! Also try long walks through appealing neighborhoods or parks, visits to museums or galleries you've been meaning to see for years, and get-togethers with other parents you've met. Some movie theaters even offer "Mommy Movies," whereby first-run films are specifically screened for parents with babes-in-arms.

It's also okay to take your baby along on a completely unnecessary appointment, allowing you to focus on you for thirty to sixty minutes out of your very, very long day. Moms, think about escaping your (likely messy) house to get your nails done, have your hair highlighted, get your brows shaped, or have a makeover at a department store cosmetic counter. If you're really concerned about bringing baby, call first—but what's the worst that can happen? He starts crying while your polish is drying? You have to feed him while waiting for your hair color to set? Worse things have happened, and usually these kinds of places are filled with females who are understanding—and may even make funny faces or otherwise entertain your little one for a few minutes.

> *"By number three, I planned ahead and organized nanny sharing with another mom for several hours a week, for a little 'mommy time.'"*
> —JANE, MOM OF THREE, AGES 10, 6 & 1

"Both moms and dads bring their babies into my salon all the time," a hairstylist friend says. "Even if they're awake, they seem to like it—there's lots to look at, mirrors to park them in front of, and good music on the stereo. It's a fun outing for them!"

[*No.*] 25 | DON'T FORGET TO
FEED the GROWN-UPS

While they might obsess about exactly how many ounces the baby is consuming on a daily basis, new parents often neglect to feed themselves. And it's more important than ever to eat well in order to keep up with the rigors of caring for an infant. You can't control your lack of sleep, for example, but you *can* control what nutrition goes into your body.

Second-time parents know that you need high-energy, healthy snacks readily available at home; this is a great responsibility to hand off to a helpful friend or family member. Load up on energy bars, nuts, hard-boiled eggs, cold sliced chicken, yogurt, peanut butter, apples, bananas, carrot sticks, and multigrain bagels. Think about items that are easy to grab and eat with one hand—if you have to stop to cut up the chicken or peel the carrots, for example, you may never get to it, especially in those first weeks.

When friends ask what they can bring over, instead of flowers or balloons ask for these kinds of items, as well as soups, stews, a rotisserie chicken, or even healthy frozen dinners from the grocery store. Think ahead about ways to keep your cupboard and fridge stocked, from setting up online delivery accounts to asking others to pick up a bag of produce at the market for you. All of this will help you stave off the temptation of eating empty fast-food calories when it's 9 P.M. and you're exhausted and starving.

New moms need protein and calories the most. If breast-feeding, she's burning an additional five hundred calories per day, and, either way, her body is working hard to recover and recalibrate from the major event of birth. She'll also be constantly thirsty, so keep bottles of water on each floor of your house and healthy juices in the fridge. Her car, diaper bag, purse, nightstand, and nursing station should all be stocked with snacks like trail mix, almonds, or energy bars, plus a water bottle.

Even when your pantry is well stocked, there's another potential roadblock to eating well in the beginning: for some reason, many newborns feel the need to holler at you every time you attempt to put some food in your mouth. We have vivid memories of our firstborn screeching in her bouncy seat while we inhaled cheeseburgers as quickly as possible. We actually felt guilty eating in front of her, because it seemed to make her so furious. Whatever sets your baby off—maybe it's the time of day, maybe it's jealousy that you get to eat something fascinating and delicious when she cannot, maybe it's something primal and inexplicable—remember to take a few moments to focus on your own health . . . even if there's an earsplitting price to pay. What are you going to do, deny your own human needs? No way. Keep your strength up and your body functioning by eating well, no matter what your baby has to say about it.

Experiment with different ways to enjoy a healthy meal during those first months when your child is not yet eating solids. Try giving her safe kitchen items to chew on and play with, or set her in front of a freshly stocked drawer of amusements. If she's not yet able to sit up, put her in an infant seat or car seat and turn on a new CD, or park her in front of a mirror or mobile. Hang some new toys from her play mat, ideally items that only come out at mealtime. If all else fails, you and your partner can take turns eating in peace—or pick certain nights to eat a nice quiet dinner together after baby's in bed. Remember, it's a stage—and soon enough, she'll be joining you at the family table. Then you'll have a host of *new* issues to distract you from your own meal!

See also, "After Delivery, Have Everything Delivered" (pg. 24) and "Earplugs Are Your Friend" (pg. 118).

[*No.*] 26 | SLEEP WHEN
the BABY SLEEPS

This might be the most-repeated advice of mothers everywhere, including your own. If it seems like you have so much to do that you mop the floor or send e-mails only while your baby naps, think about this: when you have your second baby, you will *never* be able to take this advice. You will have another child—likely a rambunctious toddler—to chase after during the hours your newborn is napping. So lie down. If you can't nap, recline and read a magazine. Watch a guilty-pleasure TV show. Or just close your eyes and meditate. Remind yourself that generation after generation of moms can't be wrong. Everything else can wait while you rest.

[No.] 27
FEED THE BABY AT *your* BEDTIME

If your baby has come to the point where she's sleeping for several hours at a stretch each night, here's a tip: you can wake her to eat before you go to bed and buy yourself more time.

Here's an example: say your infant goes to sleep around 8 P.M. and doesn't wake until 2 or 3 A.M. for a feeding, so about a six-hour stretch. Say *your* normal bedtime is 11 P.M. Try nudging her just before 11 and offer the breast or bottle. Most babies can wake just enough to eat, without becoming fully alert, so you can get some more milk in her and then just place her right back in the crib. The goal is for those six hours of sleep time to mimic your schedule more closely, meaning if she eats at 11, she might be able to go until 4 or 5 A.M., and someday (really!) 6 or 7 A.M.

Talk to your pediatrician to confirm that this is okay for your baby based on her overall feeding schedule. Then, hard as it can be to nudge a sleeping baby, give it a try. If she takes to it, you may find that you can eliminate that 3 A.M. feeding for good!

[No.] 28
YOU DON'T HAVE TO HAVE *a* BABY BOOK

"Darby's baby book is a baby drawer," admits one mom about her second-born. "I toss everything in there and figure I'll get to it sometime." It's not a bad idea, even for your first child. In this era of digital photos and video, online albums, baby blogs, and personal Web sites, is there really a need to print out, cut out, and paste in a bunch of hard-copy photos? We made a concerted effort to do this with our first,

only to feel horribly guilty when we realized (around the time number two was born) that we'd actually only made it through her first four months of life. When would we have time to scroll through the hundreds of digital photos and print them? And this was for a child who had her own pretty elaborate Web site with photos organized chronologically for easy viewing by far-flung family and friends.

Fast-forward a couple of years. Have we printed out *any* photos of our second child? Let me just say that we finally had photos for our wallets when she hit ten months old. Her version of her sister's Web site? It has pictures from the hospital, and that's it. The baby book is not happening. We've come to accept it. And as much as we'd like one to just magically appear, we know now that there are way bigger things to feel guilty about.

Second-time parents have found a variety of compromises to the traditional baby book that you might find useful the first time around.

- THE DRAWER METHOD. Dedicate a nightstand or dresser drawer to your baby. Toss in your announcement, photos, favorite shower cards, and those growth-tracking slips from your well-baby visits.

- THE BOX METHOD. Same as above, but use a shoebox, a recycled gift bag, or an accordion-style file folder. Extra credit if you find a pretty one and put your child's name on it with a Sharpie.

- THE DIGITAL METHOD. Photo Web sites make it easy to just upload your digital photos online and avoid hearing your mom complain that she hasn't seen the baby in weeks. If you have the time, you can edit them down and organize by date or event. If you have relatives who don't use a computer, it's also easy to order hard copies at the push of a button, rather than waiting until you remember to buy photo paper, print out the photos, and trim them. Again, faster than a baby book and easier to share.

- THE JOURNAL METHOD. Instead of juggling between a photo album and a baby book, we chose a leather-bound journal for each of our kids. The journals live on a side table in our living room where they are easy to grab when the mood strikes. When we remember, we jot down milestones, funny moments, thoughts and feelings, even what's going on in the world. Occasionally, we paste in a photo. Now that we have a second child, we love being able to flip back through her older sister's journal to see what she was up to at the same age. You forget so many wonderful (and frustrating) little moments as a parent, because your head is just too full. For us, skimming through what we wrote down two years ago is much more valuable than seeing a perfectly turned-out baby book.

▶ **THE E-MAIL METHOD.** Open an e-mail account for your baby (usually free with your own account) and suddenly you, your parents, and other friends and family can send messages to her with funny stories, memories, and firsts. It's usually easy to find time to dash off an e-mail—even when you're at work!—and your baby gets a wealth of different perspectives about the first year that are easily archived and shared.

[No.] 29 | THE "WITCHING HOUR"
is NOT a MYTH

Yes, your baby will have one—an hour or two at day's end when he is particularly fussy and hard to please. It will likely be around 5 to 7 P.M., not coincidentally coinciding with cocktail hour for the grown-ups. (We used to call it "unhappy hour" at our house.) It's a particular drag because it hits right when one or both parents are rushing in the door from work, eager to see the baby they've been missing all day—only to be screamed at mercilessly for no apparent reason. First-timers might succumb to it, listening to the crying evening after evening, endlessly walking and rocking the baby, feeling helpless, and even wondering if there's a medical problem. Second-timers, on the other hand, recognize it immediately and know it's a normal release mechanism for infants as they get to the end of each day. (Kind of like when you used to vent and complain over drinks after work.)

Do call your doctor or a nurse helpline if you feel your baby's discomfort is beyond typical evening fussiness; whenever he is inconsolable after all needs are met, it's important to rule out any health conditions. Also, very loud, intense, constant crying for up to three hours, three days a week, at the same time of day (often accompanied by clenched fists and curled legs) may be considered colic, for which your doctor might have other advice. Clean bill of health and baby is still a pill? Then you're just part of the witching-hour club.

When you are at your wit's end, think about two things: First, every parent in the world is dealing with this at the same time, and they are all as frazzled about it as you are—can you feel the global solidarity? Second, understand that this is one of many parenting moments when fixing the problem may be impossible. It's something your baby has to go through, and all you can do is be there for him.

Thankfully, babies usually outgrow this by the three-month mark (although this time of day is rarely ever a great one for babies and toddlers). Until then, give the following ideas a try to hopefully ease the pandemonium.

▶ **MUSIC.** Play everything from hard rock to country to soul, and crank it to eleven. Some babies also respond well to white noise (on an inexpensive noise machine or your vacuum) or static (on your old-school radio).

▶ **QUIET.** If music is having the wrong effect, try the opposite—rock him in a quiet, dark room with little stimulation.

▶ **GET OUTSIDE.** Fresh, cool air can sometimes surprise babies out of their fuss. Don't go through the hassle of getting him all bundled up; even a quick step onto the porch in his pj's can do the trick, no matter the weather.

▶ **MOTION.** Walk with baby snug in a carrier (around the block or even up and down the stairs), bounce him on an exercise ball, drive him in the car, or rock him in different holds. Even sitting with him on an active clothes washer can work—and you'll be multitasking!

▸ **SKIN-TO-SKIN CONTACT.** Try holding baby tight against your bare skin.

▸ **CHANGE THE SCENE.** There's nothing like a change of scenery to snap kids out of a mood, whether they're four weeks or four years old. Go to a different part of the house, tour the garage, show him something packed deep in a closet that he's never seen before.

> *"When trying to soothe a fussy baby,*
> *remember that this is one time when people's*
> *ridiculous advice might actually help you.*
> *As long as it's not physically dangerous,*
> *you may as well try it. And as you struggle*
> *along, you'll get to know your baby better—*
> *you'll see whether she prefers rocking*
> *or bouncing, hard rock or easy listening,*
> *darkness or bright light."*
>
> —ANNA, MOM OF TWO, AGES 5 & 3

Some babies go through tougher and longer witching hours than others, and it seems just to be the luck of the draw. While second-time parents don't have a solution to it, they do approach it differently: they don't necessarily listen to every decibel of it. If your baby is fed, burped, and dry but simply not able to take any comfort from you during witching hour night after night, you *can* put him in his crib or play yard and get away from the ruckus for a while. Experienced parents do it all the time.

"We just can't take it some evenings, because it's right in the middle of our family dinnertime," explains one mom of three. "If I can't settle the baby down, she goes in her crib upstairs while we eat."

See also, "You Can Turn Off the Baby Monitor" (pg. 78), "Earplugs Are Your Friend" (pg. 118), and "You Can Let Your Baby Cry" (pg. 127).

DAD MIGHT FEEL
LEFT OUT *at* FIRST

"I'm the one who had to give birth," the new moms out there might be thinking, *"and I'm supposed to worry about my husband now?"* Well, yes. Let's not forget about him. With all the mom-baby attachment during the first few weeks, especially if Mom is breast-feeding, Dad gets very little physical bonding with the baby. Plus, when new babies aren't eating, they are often sleeping and therefore hands-off.

If he was lucky enough to swing a chunk of paternity leave, Dad might be in the unexpected position of being home in the middle of the day with nothing to do. If, like many men, he likes to busy himself with a project, he may find himself at loose ends. On top of this, he simply wants to be involved with his new child but feels stymied at every turn. This will make him unhappy. Moms might read this the wrong way, wondering, "What's his problem? He's not the one who's feeding this kid every two hours!" You might even get angry when you see him doing non-baby-related tasks or resentful to hear him peacefully snoring when you come back to bed after yet another feeding.

> *"Dads can get frustrated when trying to help with bottle-feedings, especially when the baby refuses . . . but remember, a baby has never starved when there's a full bottle next to him. Persevere, and the baby will learn to adapt."*
> —SCOTT, DAD OF TWO, AGES 7 & 4

The second time around, dads are more prepared for life with a newborn and have learned how to help without frustrating themselves or their partners. Plus, fathers often take on the important duty of being in charge of the older child, which gives them a better sense of purpose.

So, how to bring Dad deeper into things with your first baby? Make sure he gets plenty of time holding, bathing, diapering, and dressing the baby. Let him walk around with the infant in the sling, take her for a walk in the stroller, or zip out with her to Home Depot while you rest. Explain the benefits of skin-on-skin contact, and have him spend time with baby on his bare chest, a really delicious treat. Dads also seem to have a special chromosome that allows easy tandem napping on the couch while golf plays on TV in the background. Whatever works, encourage all the bonding you can.

For example, in our house, our first baby woke up around 5 A.M. for a period of time, but she could go back to sleep if you held her. This became Dad's job, and he embraced it, setting up a comfy nest on our living room recliner before going to bed at night and then whisking the baby downstairs at dawn, cuddling there with her for an hour or two. It's still one of his favorite memories.

Second-time moms also know to put dads to work. If he's the type that really needs to be useful, designate him point person on baby-related jobs that can be done while you're nursing or the baby is sleeping. He can tackle some early childproofing, laundry, dishes, shopping, or cooking. He might have a flair for whipping up casseroles that you never knew he possessed! Dad also might be in charge of photography, videos, the baby announcements, thank-you cards, or starting a baby Web site. He can compare prices online for major pieces like cribs and strollers, create your new will, set up your baby's college fund, troll online sites for bargains, or place an ad for childcare help.

Many dads find that they enjoy the baby more and feel more useful after the first three months. If you suspect that might be the case for you, you might consider something a lot of second-time parents do—have Dad take his paternity leave later, or split the time between now and later, if he and his employer can arrange it. Your house will probably be full right after the baby is born anyway, with grandparents and other visitors descending on your firstborn. After your mom has gone home and the baby is awake for longer stretches of time, it might be an ideal time for Dad to be home and for you to have some family time together.

[No.] 31 | DON'T FEEL GUILTY ABOUT
CALLING the DOCTOR

Experienced parents know that one of the most important things to ask when you choose a pediatrician is whether there is a 24/7 nurse advice line for you to call with any manner of big or small questions. You see, as much as we advocate not sweating the small stuff, that advice is much easier to follow when your mind can be put at ease with a single phone call.

> *"The first time around, it seemed like I called the doctor too soon or too late when the baby seemed sick. I looked like either a worrywart or a negligent mother. The second time, I stopped worrying about what the doctor thought of me and listened to my intuition instead."*
>
> —SARAH, MOM OF TWO, AGES 8 & 6

Is your baby tugging at his ear repeatedly? Did he tip over backward while trying to sit up? Is he whacking his head against the side of the crib every night? Does he just not seem himself today? Second-time parents may glide through a lot of this stuff—but on the flip side, since they worry a lot less about how things look or who they're bothering, they don't hesitate to ask when something is outside their comfort zone. Hopefully, with a well-worded response from your doctor's office, you will learn to glide through it as well. Whatever is bugging you, you'll be more likely to relax about it when a friendly RN tells you warning signs to watch for, none of which your baby has. Remember, calling does not make you seem like a crazy, overprotective novice. It is a means to an end: a more relaxed and confident you.

[No.] 32 | ## BABIES DON'T NEED THEIR BOTTLES *or* FOOD HEATED

Did you get one of those cute little bottle or baby-food warmers as a shower gift? Return it. Second-time parents have learned that when you begin giving your baby a bottle or baby food, you should offer it at room temperature (or even cold).

"My friends were shocked when they heard that I didn't mess around with heating up bottles. It hadn't occurred to them to try to give their babies a cold bottle," says a mom of three. "I figured it out by the second baby, and it's so much less work!"

Not only do you save yourself a step—and that step can seem infinitely long when your baby is screaming—you make it less stressful to feed her on the go. If you can take a bottle of breast milk out of a cooler in the car or hotel room and pop it in her mouth, everyone's happy. Think of it this way: if she truly balks after repeated tries with cold bottles, you can always start warming them up . . . but it's hard to go the other way once you've gotten your little one used to warm.

ENDEAVOR TO
KEEP it SIMPLE

Second-timers are all about efficiency. They've learned that if you begin by keeping every routine with your baby as simple as possible, you can always add more complexity if it's needed. It's harder to go the other way. For example, you might start with a fifteen-minute bedtime routine, rather than a sixty-minute one, and see if it works—you can always make it longer when you have time and feel like it. See where we're going here?

> *"While I think sleep routines are very important, with our first daughter we had a routine that involved her falling asleep to an ocean-sounds CD every night. Even when we went to Hawaii and could hear the real ocean we brought the CD player and CD! When it finally wore out we bought a new one, which unfortunately had foghorns and seagulls so that was the end of the ocean. My daughter didn't even notice! We didn't even start down that path with the second."*
>
> —PAULA, MOM OF TWO, AGES 8 & 6

Let's think of a variety of time-consuming rituals first-timers often do automatically that are really, truly, not necessary. A daily bath? No. Diaper checks every time your baby squawks in the night? No. Staying with your baby until he's sound asleep at every bedtime? No. Making your own baby food? No. Sterilizing everything within an inch of its life? No. Separating the baby's laundry? No. Warming up baby food and bottles? No.

Rest assured, it's okay to do all the things you want to do, especially when you are taking a limited maternity leave and you've got this one amazing newborn all to yourself. It's a time to devote all available energy to your baby—and nothing else seems important. So if there are time-consuming routines that you know are unnecessary but bring you both joy, go right ahead. Take your time. Sing twelve songs at naptime. Do baths every night. Just realize that if you keep up this pace for the entire first year, it may be hard to backpedal and get him to accept less.

If and when you find that you're ready to scale back a few things, out of desire or necessity, ask yourself which routines you and your child are enjoying the most and which seem like they could be streamlined without much issue. Edit the least-favorite routines first, and see how it goes. Your reward might well be a few more minutes of well-deserved downtime for yourself—and a more adaptable child.

[*No.*] 34 | MAKE PEACE
WITH the PACIFIER

Other parenting books will go on for pages about the pacifier, addressing all possible concerns first-timers might have. Does it hinder language? Complicate breast-feeding? Affect teeth? Is it a parental crutch? Is it politically correct? Second-time parents, on the other hand, have only a simple answer to a single question: *Does it seem to help your baby soothe herself?* If so, use it. If not, don't. When it stops working or no longer seems necessary—for example, if your baby finds fingers to suck on instead—get rid of it.

Some babies want the pacifier only for sleeping; others all day long. Some babies only want it during the newborn weeks; others have to have it pried away from them (with elaborate stories about the pacifier fairy) at age four. Authors of books will have a variety of opinions, as will all other parents you ask. You simply won't know how reliant your baby will be on it, and what feels right to you, until you're in the thick of it. Pretty much the only thing everyone agrees on is that you can't rely on the pacifier as a "plug" to quiet your crying baby in lieu of trying to figure out what's wrong.

Whether or not to offer a pacifier and when to take it away are personal decisions for your family. Instead of relying on all of your peers' experiences, do what feels right, and if you need an objective opinion, ask your pediatrician.

[No.] 35 | DON'T BE A SLAVE TO the BABY'S SCHEDULE

With our first baby, feedings and naptimes were like clockwork; we knew exactly what time we wanted to be home to nurse or get our daughter to sleep, and we didn't waver from it. As new parents, we liked having that very rigid structure in a world that had turned all topsy-turvy. You might feel that way too. But we're here to remind you that although babies do like predictability, you don't have to be a slave to the schedule—nor do you have to throw it out the window to show you can still be spontaneous, although this seems less common in first-timers. Basically, being extreme on either side of the coin will increase your stress. Instead, shoot for an approximate daily schedule and know that you can diverge from it as life intervenes.

> *"Kids will sleep when they need to sleep, eat when they need to eat, and cry when they need to cry."*
> —GORD, DAD OF TWO, AGES 10 & 7

For instance, say you want to take a walk around the lake that will take an hour and a half, but your baby is due to eat in an hour. Don't skip the walk—instead, see if he can make it a little longer today (and be prepared to stop and feed him if you really have to). If you're going someplace you might be uncomfortable breast-feeding, do a preemptive feeding at home, even though it's not time yet. Know that it's okay if sometimes your baby naps in the car or stroller when you can't be home right on time—if the sleep is not as good as in the crib, he'll make up for it later. Remember, second (and third, and fourth) babies live their lives at the mercy of their older siblings, and rarely can they have every nap and meal in the exact same spot or at the exact same time. Loosen up the reins a bit, and you'll probably be surprised to find that your baby does just fine, even with a skipped nap or a less-than-ideal feeding—and that you feel more at ease too.

[*No.*] 36 | DRESS YOUR BABY IN
WHATEVER'S EASIEST

The great thing about being a baby is that you look cute (and appropriate) in anything. Pj's at the grocery store? Sure! Polka-dot top with striped pants? Naturally! And in the summer? A simple T-shirt (or nothing but a diaper!) is a perfectly fine ensemble. So put aside all those fussy outfits you got as gifts, no matter how adorable they are. If they require thirty extra seconds to put on, especially once your baby is mobile, you will continue to shove them to the back of the drawer and reach for the same soft onesies day after day. (And here's a tip—if she hasn't peed or spit up on it yet, it's fine to wear again.)

SECOND-TIMER TIP

*Zippers are a million times easier
than snaps, especially for one-piece pajamas
that might have to come off in the night
while baby's limbs are flailing.*

If you've always been the type who likes outfits to be just so, you might as well relax your expectations when it comes to your baby. You see, someday this child will insist on wearing a tutu and rain boots, even to your sister's wedding—so you'd better get used to it now. Don't feel guilty about the complicated outfits with the tags still on them; you can re-gift them or donate them to charity. Meanwhile, experienced parents understand that if it's comfy, reasonably weather-appropriate, and has a zipper, then it's the right thing to wear, no matter the occasion.

66

67

[*No.*] **37**

EVERYTHING—
EVERYTHING— is a STAGE

What is driving you crazy about your baby right now? Is he needing to constantly be held, crying in protest every time you put him down? Is he refusing the breast or bottle? Is he flinging his food onto the floor repeatedly? Is he flipping himself over in his sleep and startling himself awake? Is he unable to go to sleep unless someone is cradling him? Does he refuse to smile? Is he just crying and crying and crying?

Babies can be the most inexplicable, infuriating creatures on the planet. There are times you'll think you want to throw him out the window, or, at the very least, get into your car solo and never look back. (It's a good thing they're cute, right?) When you are at the end of your rope, remember something simple yet vital that all second-time parents know, deep in their hearts, even at the darkest moments: *this too shall pass.*

> *"You don't need to 'master' any stage or age. You just need to survive it. There is always another phase to enjoy and to challenge you just around the corner."*
>
> —ELIZABETH, MOM OF TWO, AGES 1 & 1

Second-timers, through the lens of their experience, have fully embraced the understanding that everything is a stage with kids. Whatever issue is driving you bonkers today, you can guarantee it will end—only to be replaced by another one. If your baby is not eating well one week, next week he'll be feeding great but not sleeping. If your baby hates baths right now, in a few days he'll love them. Screaming at Daddy every time he comes in? Next month, Dad'll be the recipient of his first proud wave. The rub is that the good times are stages too. When you're thrilled to find your baby particularly settled for a few days, sleeping well, smiling and content—revel in it. It's not permanent. Phases can be long or short, adorable or exasperating, but they begin in babyhood and never stop. The only thing they have in common is that they're temporary.

> *"After having three kids, I've finally released all my guilty feelings over my firstborn. I've realized that even though I probably didn't do all the 'right' things with my first, she has still grown up to be the most amazing ten-year-old, and I wouldn't trade her for all the money in the world."*
>
> —JANE, MOM OF THREE, AGES 10, 6 & 1

Of course, when you're in the thick of it, you find it hard to believe any of this. But the day will come when you and your partner will look at each other and say, *Hey, it's been a couple of days since he did _____, hasn't it?* You'll be so absorbed in what new thing he's doing that it might take a bit of time to register that the loathed behavior you'd come to accept has disappeared. It may come back, and then go away, and then come back. But rejoice in the days when it's gone.

You may also find that when you come out on the other side of one of these stages, a new maturity has emerged in your child. Sometimes a particularly fussy stage means some major development is happening, physically, mentally, or emotionally. So try to watch for—and enjoy—the new child blossoming in front of you when a stage ends. You might suddenly see a new tooth, a new ability to move an object from one hand to another, a new sound. Your little person has been working hard and enduring some discomfort, and here is the reward: he's growing up.

[*No.*]
38

YOU MAY NOT LOVE
your BABY'S "LOVEY"

Second-timers fall into two basic camps when it comes to advice on "loveys" (those beloved soft dolls, animals, or blankies that give some babies untold comfort—and can cause major meltdowns if missing):

 *Those who recommend not allowing baby to attach to one particular lovey. They claim that it's too much trouble to hunt high and low for that special something all the time, to remember to take it everywhere, and to replace it if lost. Instead, these parents suggest putting a variety of blankets and animals into rotation in the crib in hopes that any soft cuddly thing will do.* *continues ›*

2 *Those who love loveys for their ability to instantly soothe.*
Folks in this camp encourage the use of one that you
approve of—namely one that is small (i.e., easy to take
everywhere), inexpensive, and readily replaceable. If baby
starts to attach to something troublesome (a queen-size
sheet, for example, or a limited-edition Beanie Baby), they
advise to wean her off it tout de suite *and offer a substitute.*

Granted, some of this may be out of your control. Some babies just attach more strongly to objects than others, and their reasoning, as always, can be inexplicable. (Why the huge, hard-shelled electronic turtle with the battery pack and the broken leg? Why not this adorable soft bunny? Here, sweetie, just feel the bunny, it's so much nicer . . .) But you *can* encourage (or discourage) the use of the lovey if you decide where you stand early on. Remember, whatever you end up with, your child might be the type who requires you to bring it to the doctor's office, onto the plane, and into restaurants, so be mindful of what your baby seeks out as her special object—and if it's not okay with you, put it out of sight and offer a better alternative. (Luckily, out of sight is usually out of mind the first year; after that, she'll demand it no matter how deep you bury it in the closet.) At the end of the day, if your little one does become attached to that one special thing, do yourself a favor and buy two.

[*No.*] 39 | PLAYING WITH YOUR BABY
may not COME NATURALLY

"It took me a long time to admit this," a mom of two confesses, "but I'm not really good at playing. I'm good at reading books and doing puzzles now that my daughter is older. But just open-ended play for hours on end? Especially the first year, when she didn't really *do* anything? Not my strong suit." If you ever look at your baby at 8 A.M. and wonder what the heck you're supposed to do with him all day, you're not alone.

> *"Play lots. It may not seem like it when your kid's screaming in the middle of the night, but they do grow up pretty fast. Don't get caught up in making sure your house is always clean, that toys are always put away, or that the laundry room doesn't always look like a bomb just went off. Play as much as you can, if for no other reason than your kid's toys are probably way cooler than the ones you had when you were their age."*
>
> —GORD, DAD OF TWO, AGES 10 & 7

Some new parents find themselves mesmerized watching their kids repeatedly press the button on the jack-in-the-box, while others are checking the clock. For most of us, our patience and energy for play depends on the day, our mood, and what's on our minds. All parents have moments when we'd rather be doing something other than entertaining our children—as much as we love them. But as a first-timer, if you find you are almost always antsy, feeling like you should be accomplishing tasks instead of quietly playing with your baby, do try to let yourself relax into it. Remember, it's a completely different mind-set than anything you've done before, and very different than the years of results-driven school and work that we're trained for. There is no goal here, except quality time with your baby. That can be hard to get used to. Practice makes perfect, though, and by setting aside blocks of time to just lie on the floor with your baby and play peek-a-boo, flip through a stack of board books, or play-act with stuffed animals, you will begin to discover what makes your baby tick—and what you enjoy doing with him as well. That said, you might find that extended periods of play just aren't suited to your personality or temperament. In that case, find ways to "play" while doing other things: Set out an assortment of pots, pans, and Tupperware for baby to interact with and plop him on the floor (or put a younger infant in his infant seat) while you cook or do dishes, talking or singing to him. Give him paper to crumple while you pay bills, write thank-yous, or place orders from catalogs. Offer an assortment of scarves and set him in front of your full-length mirror while you put laundry away, get dressed, or clean your closet. And, of course, take him on all your errands, explaining things to him along the way.

No matter how much of an achiever you are, do try to have some time each day when the phone and PDA are turned off, your chores are on the back burner, and you are giving total eye contact and consideration to your baby. Small as they are, they know the difference, and when offered your undivided attention, they will almost always reward you with some heartwarming and unexpected expression or reaction that will take your breath away. It just might be enough to make you want to play all the way until dinnertime.

[No.] 40 | LET YOUR PARTNER
DO THINGS HIS WAY

Yes, we're talking primarily to the moms here. That's on purpose. Why? Because it tends to be the new mom who looks over the dad's shoulder, offering helpful and unsolicited advice on how to do everything exactly as she would—from changing a diaper to entertaining the baby to mixing a bottle of formula. Needless to say, this type of micromanagement is not only unnecessary, it is usually unappreciated as well. It can cause resentment and frustration during what is already an emotionally charged time for any couple. And regardless of Dad's reaction, in the end it only defeats the purpose of having him do his share.

"I was hosting friends and their new baby, and the mom asked her husband to change the baby's diaper since we were in the middle of a conversation," a friend recalls. "Then she followed him upstairs and checked on him anyway." The irony? After lecturing him on how the diaper was on too tight, she had to eat crow when he explained the diaper she was criticizing hadn't even been changed yet—so it was the diaper *she* had put on that was supposedly unacceptable.

Second-time moms, on the other hand, are so eager to grab any help they can get that they tend to be more relaxed about people doing things their way. If Dad, Grandma, or a babysitter is willing to do the next feeding/bath/diaper change, Mom is all for it—and, in fact, unless someone is screaming bloody murder, she probably won't give the technique a second thought. The result is more empowerment and interaction for spouses, friends, and family members—and a child who doesn't expect everything to be done just the way Mom does.

Of course, this doesn't mean you can't help out your spouse by explaining tricks you've discovered and lessons you've learned by trial and error with your child—something Dad hasn't had as much of if he's gone back to work before you. But as with any unsolicited advice, there's a wrong way ("Don't just dump water on his head! He hates that! Hold him like this instead! Why is it so cold in here?") and a right way.

"I found that the best time to bring up any suggestion was later, say, over dinner or when we're chatting with other parents about how they do things," says a mom of two boys. "If I tried to give him constructive criticism in the moment, it became a battle—and an excuse for him to give up and let me do it." That isn't a desirable result for anyone.

So if your suggestion isn't an immediate safety imperative, hold your tongue, wait for a good moment, and finesse your delivery. If your spouse had a hard time doing the bath his way, for example, try phrasing your advice like this: *I really struggle getting Sally's hair washed too. It's not easy. Do you know what I found has worked this week? I hold a toy really high over my head—then when she looks up, I rinse her hair with my other hand*. Our guess is that will go over a lot better than bursting into the bathroom at the first sound of crying and demanding to know what's going on.

The same lessons apply to other caregivers, whether paid babysitters or visiting relatives. While you will naturally want to give copious advice and tell them all the quirky little things you do—exactly how you rock the baby, what washcloth you use, where she likes to be tickled—it's important for them to know that they don't have to imitate you step by step. Other people in your baby's life need to find their own way with her and their own routines within the guidelines you've set for them. Does it really matter to your baby whether the pajamas come before or after the bottle, for example, as long as both steps happen? Probably not. There will be a certain way Grandma holds him, a different song that your babysitter sings in the tub, and eventually these will become fun for her to look forward to when she sees these people. You might even learn some new tips and tricks to use yourself.

[*No.*] **41**

EMBRACE THE
POWER *of* "NO"

A dad we met recently, whose third child is on the way, recalls: "With the first baby, you kid yourself that life is going to be the same, and you try to keep it up, say yes to invitations, travel . . . by the second, you give up that charade." In our experience, the sooner you get your mind around this, the less disappointed you'll be. Second-time parents have learned that it doesn't make you a failure or a bore to start saying no to things—whether major ventures like a cross-country wedding or a ski trip with your childless friends, or even small-scale local plans that just don't work well for some reason. It makes you a parent.

Now, we believe in babysitters and also endeavor to take the family to events that mean a lot to us, but we have also learned the power of saying no. Keep in mind that you don't even have to explain this answer, or justify it, or provide long-winded explanations about naps or ear infections; instead, just practice saying, "Sorry, we can't make it this time." Period.

You'll discover that it's a key parenting survival skill to know what's worth doing and what's not worth doing—and to accept that all decisions now involve the needs, wants, and comfort of everyone in the family. For example, we learned the hard way with our firstborn that a trip to a rustic beach cabin wasn't the best choice for our new baby, and that Mom or Dad might've had more fun going solo to that faraway wedding. So we now pick and choose with care, understanding that there will be times when we're really disappointed to have to miss something. In hindsight, we rarely have wished we had said yes to something that really seemed like too much effort for our family.

We know parents who do everything with their babies—attend late-night concerts, take cruises, backpack across Europe—and figure the baby will sleep when he's tired enough and everyone will be just fine. There are folks who say yes to every opportunity and wear this like a badge of honor. And maybe you'll be one of them. But probably not. And that's okay. Because sometimes, saying no to certain things means saying yes to the well-being of your family (not to mention your own sanity).

[*No.*] 42 | YOUR LIFE IS SUPPOSED
to be DIFFERENT

Do you feel panicked that your life will never look like it used to? Afraid that you may never be able to keep up the same rate of work, exercise, travel, socializing, and other activities that you enjoyed before baby? Concerned that you aren't giving your friends or partner the same energy as you did when you were childless? Before you fall into despair, or try desperately to do it all, it may help to remember that your life is *supposed* to be different now. You have entered a new stage; a new stage *shouldn't* be the same. There would be something wrong if it was.

> *"Your kids will worship you, so don't be a loser. As kids grow, they want to like what you like, act how you act, and do what you do. Make sure their main role model isn't a lazy sloth who's angry about life and bitter at the world. We've got enough of those people on the planet already."*
>
> —GORD, DAD OF TWO, AGES 10 & 7

We remember a single friend saying to us, a few months after our first was born, "Aren't you getting anxious to get your life back?" And actually, it was the *question* that made us anxious. What did that mean? Where had that previous life gone? When were we supposed to get it back, and how? By our second child, there was a new understanding: it's not about getting your old life back. This *is* your life. The old one doesn't exist anymore. And that's okay—that's why you did this thing in the first place!

[*No.*] 43 | YOU CAN IGNORE
YOUR PARENTS

"Just put a little rice cereal in his bottle; he'll sleep better."

"No one in *our* family ever had [insert habit or health condition here]!"

"What do you mean, she doesn't use a pacifier?"

"Just put him in front of the TV—it's relaxing!"

"You're not nursing?"

"You're *still* nursing?"

Oh, there's nothing like becoming a parent to make your own parents really get on your nerves. Savor the irony. Once you have your first baby, you may be surprised at the frequency with which the new grandparents offer you unsolicited (and sometimes questionable) advice. They might make passive-aggressive comments, wonder aloud at your way of doing things, and even be downright critical of your decisions on any number of personal parenting choices—from going back to work to breast- versus bottle-feeding to choosing to sleep with your baby. It may get to the point where even having them in the house causes your hackles to go up, ready to pounce and refute any token of wisdom they offer. And as much as we'd like to lay all blame squarely on them, we have to point out that there is no one on Earth more defensive than a first-time parent.

It's understandable. You are trying so hard to do everything right. You are scared. You are fiercely protective. You are also extraordinarily tired and overwhelmed. And at least one of you has some crazy hormones surging through her body. All this can be an explosive combination if someone dares to offer you another way of doing things . . . especially your own parents. Who do they think they are?

Relax. Second-time parents might still have issues with their parents' advice, but they are more apt to let it roll off their backs. (After all, they've managed to get at least one child through babyhood relatively unscathed, so they know they're doing something right.) Try to remember that, with rare exception, your parents are truly only trying to help—and they want what's best for your baby too. That's not to say they are always right, especially when reminiscing about their own days as a new parent, which they cannot help but do. The truth is, there is no way your mom or dad possibly remembers every detail from your own infancy—you will find this out when your child is two and you have no memory whatsoever of when she got her first tooth—so take their recollections with a grain of salt. Plus, times have changed. They are offering thirty-year-old advice, when babies stayed in playpens, moms smoked through pregnancy, and there was no such thing as a car seat. Both science and popular opinion about baby-raising are always evolving, and you can't expect your parents to be up on the latest research or trends. Believe it or not, someday you'll be in their shoes, and things you're doing now will be pooh-poohed by your own children!

Until then, try to keep this all in perspective. Remember that you are in charge of your own household and your baby, and you don't need to justify everything you do to your parents. If you are not open to discussion on a particularly charged subject, say so by simply stating that this is what you and your partner have decided is best for your own family, a response that's hard for even your parents to contest. For other day-to-day matters, don't let yourself be so irritated or defensive that you refuse to hear any nuggets of truth or insight Grandma or Grandpa might have. They *did* do this before, after all, and you turned out pretty well.

In the end, if you find you simply don't agree with them, just do what second-time parents do: briskly nod; say, "Thanks, I'll think about that"; and move on.

[No.] 44 | ## YOU CAN TURN OFF
the BABY MONITOR

One of the key discoveries that second-time parents have made is that babies make a lot of noise—and, believe it or not, it is not essential that you hear every last sound.

Our first baby snuffled and snorted through the night for her first eight weeks while we slept fitfully six inches away from her. We quickly learned that most of the time she was asleep and needed nothing, yet we endured the noise night after night. From getting up the couple of times she actually needed to be fed to listening to all the commotion in between, there was hardly a chance to get any deep sleep at all. And you expect that with a newborn, so we didn't think twice about it. When she reached the three-month mark, we proudly took the plunge and moved her into her own room just across the hall . . . but because we used a monitor religiously, we *still* heard every little REM-time grunt or rustle.

Why did we put up with this? We cannot tell you. (We also charted every single dirty diaper and feeding during those first months, and that clearly wasn't necessary either.) But here's the thing: by the time you have your second baby, instead of worrying about how to ensure you hear her, you worry about how to ensure you *don't* hear her. We did keep our second baby in our room for the first few weeks, but we quickly shuttled her off to another floor the moment she was able to go several hours without a feeding. We remember that night well. We shut off the monitor, opened our bedroom door, and knew that if she truly howled, we'd hear her. (As our pediatrician noted, "There's nothing wrong with making sure she's *really* hungry before feeding her—that's how she learns to go longer and longer between nursings.") Sure, it meant going down a flight of stairs for the middle-of-the-night feeding, but it was well worth it—because for those precious hours in between, we couldn't hear her random moans and rustlings, and we slept deeply. And she seemed to sleep more soundly too (as far as we know, anyway). Our whole family began to function a little better. From that moment on, we haven't used a monitor unless we're actually leaving the house to play in the backyard during her naptime. Trust us, unless you live in some sort of mansion where your baby sleeps in a separate wing, if your baby needs you, you will hear her loud and clear.

Whether you're comfortable getting rid of the monitor altogether, there are times when you truly *must* turn it off: when you've determined you're not going in to get her. Many first-time parents, after making the commitment to let the baby cry for ten minutes, sit right next to the monitor with rising blood pressure. Why torture yourself? Your baby's wail will get under your skin like no other sound in the universe. The only way to give yourself a break, and make it to that ten-minute mark, is to avoid hearing it.

Turn off the monitor. Remind yourself that your baby is safe in his crib and wants for nothing, repeat the mantra that babies sometimes just need to cry, and then get out of earshot. Set a timer and go out to your deck or yard, into your garage, or even into the shower—any place where the sound is muffled. Earplugs or music headphones are not a bad idea if your home offers no good escape. Ideally, have a refreshing beverage, a mindless magazine, a trusted parent you can call, or another diversion. After ten minutes, check the monitor and listen for your baby. If her cries are slowing down, turn it off again and check back in another ten. If she is ramping up, go in to pat her back or proceed with whatever routine you are following, then leave again and turn off the monitor. Repeat. When it's your bedtime, open your bedroom door and don't use the monitor. You might actually get a few hours of well-deserved sleep and see your smiling baby, no worse for the wear, in the morning. Hallelujah!

See also, "Earplugs Are Your Friend" (pg. 118) and "You Can Let Your Baby Cry" (pg. 127).

[No.] 45 | DON'T WORRY ABOUT BEING PRODUCTIVE right NOW

It's a whole new world, Mom and Dad. You are no longer judged on how much you cross off your to-do list—you are accomplishing a major feat each day that you parent this new person. And boy, do the days just disappear—you will likely look at the clock some afternoons and wonder where the time could've gone, especially if you didn't even leave the house. Yet even during maternity and paternity leave, some personality types feel as if they should be getting *something* done. Second-time parents look at it a little differently—you *are* getting something done, and hey, if you and your baby have been fed and are reasonably clean, you've done quite enough, thank you.

So if you don't get around to what you had intended—a trip to the hardware store, clearing out a closet, pulling the weeds in the yard—don't sweat it. Or if your list of Saturday household chores is still pinned to the fridge on Monday, so be it. Tomorrow, or next weekend, or the weekend after that will be here soon enough. Some days, both you and baby may just need to stay in and chill. That's perfectly okay. After all, when your second baby comes, you won't have the option!

See also, "It's Okay for You and Your Baby to 'Do Nothing' All Day" (pg. 106).

[No.] 46 | DON'T OVERPACK FOR
EVERY little OUTING

It's great to be prepared, but sometimes packing up your baby for an outing can make leaving the house seem like more trouble than it's worth. First-time moms often make this more stressful, time-consuming, and cumbersome than it needs to be. With all the other ways your body is being taxed every day, you really don't need to be a pack mule. If you can't imagine walking around the block without a fully stocked diaper bag, it's time to downsize. Here are some tips:

▶ Instead of a giant diaper bag, use a small, comfortable tote; messenger bag; or fabric pouch with a cross-strap for short outings. All you need is a diaper or two, a small zip-top bag of wipes, your cell phone and ID, and a few bucks in case you need a coffee or a cookie. (For newborns, add one rolled-up onesie in case of a diaper blowout.)

▶ If you're pushing a stroller, keep these essentials plus a small blanket or changing pad in the stroller basket, and take off with your shoulders unencumbered.

▸ If you will be out during mealtime and your baby is on formula, instead of lugging a full bottle and ice pack, bring your powdered formula premeasured in one of those snack cups with compartments, then just mix with water when (and if) you need it. See also, "Babies Don't Need Their Bottles or Food Heated" (pg. 62).

▸ If your baby is eating solids, skip the mess of baby food for one meal and just bring along a banana, whole-wheat bagel, or other finger foods. If you're going to another household (or a restaurant), you'll find enough baby-friendly foods to cobble together a meal.

▸ If you're driving, keeping a few essentials stocked in your car will allow you to take off quickly without packing so much in your bag. See also, "Keep Your Car Stocked," next.

▸ If you're going to the houses of other parents, or even to baby classes, playgroups, or parent meetings, you don't need to bring all your gear—there will always be someone to borrow from, and things like diapers or emergency clothing don't have to be the exact right size to work in a pinch.

"There's just no need for the big expensive diaper bag. It's not only hard on your back, it's just a lot of little straps and pockets and pouches where everything can get lost."

—ELIZA, MOM OF TWO, AGES 4 & 3

Remember, if worse comes to worst, you can go home or buy or borrow what you need. In general, parents are happy to share diapers, wipes, or snacks with a fellow parent in need.

[*No.*] 47 | ## KEEP YOUR

CAR STOCKED

By keeping a few things in a cardboard box on the floor of your backseat, you have a constant insurance policy. Open your diaper bag at the restaurant to find it's packed with everything except diapers? Zip out to the car and you're all set. Here's what should be in your box at all times (and don't forget to restock!):

▶ Five diapers

▶ Full-size pack of wipes (to clean hands, faces, and clothing, as well as bottoms)

{
SECOND-TIMER TIP

Unless you know you're going to be coming right home, always put your stroller in the trunk of your car—just in case. If your baby falls asleep, it might be a perfect time to run some errands or take a walk—and you do not want to lug that infant car seat around.
}

▶ Hand sanitizer

▶ Bottle of water (for drinking, dealing with messes, or mixing formula)

▶ Baby blanket (for warmth or to use as a changing pad)

- Nonperishable snack (if baby's on solids), such as a couple of wrapped teething biscuits or zwieback toast

- Nonperishable snack for you (like an energy bar or trail mix)

- Sustenance for one meal if your baby is not breast-feeding exclusively (i.e., bottle and dry formula and/or one jar of baby food with spoon and bib)

{

SECOND-TIMER TIP

If you don't have a camera phone, consider keeping a disposable camera in your car, stroller, or diaper bag for capturing adorable moments.

}

- Change of clothes for baby (make sure it's size- and season-appropriate as the months pass)

- Change of breast pads and shirt for you (if breast-feeding)

- Towel (for any number of things, from drying off playground swings to mopping up spit-up; this is a great way to recycle your ratty dishtowels)

- Extra pacifier, if your baby uses one

- Extra favorite toy, book, or lovey

{

SECOND-TIMER TIP

Use luggage tags to keep your child's name and emergency contact information on your diaper bag, stroller, and car seat.

}

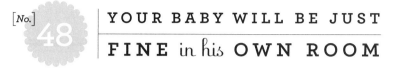

YOUR BABY WILL BE JUST
FINE *in his* OWN ROOM

When our friend brought her first son home, she tried her best to wedge a portable crib into her small bedroom. "Everyone I knew had their baby in the same room," she says. "I didn't even really think I had a choice." After five weeks of having to practically climb over it to get into bed, she moved him across the hall and—surprise, surprise—he was fine. In fact, everyone slept better. The second time around? "He was in his room from the first day," she says. "And to this day, both kids are very comfortable sleeping on their own, with the door closed. We're happy to have adult time from 7:30 P.M. on, every night—with our room and the rest of the house to ourselves."

> *"When you transition your baby to his own crib, consider putting the mattress at the lowest setting, rather than the highest, from the start. Every time the mattress height is adjusted, it can be an adjustment for baby too. We avoided tears the second time around by setting the crib once and only once."*
>
> —ELIZA, MOM OF TWO, AGES 4 & 3

Whether you put baby in his own room will depend on your baby's health and disposition, your personal feelings, and also your floor plan. We know parents who slept in the same room with their child until past his first birthday, because otherwise he would have been on another floor, and they just didn't feel comfortable with that. We know other parents who put their babies in their own rooms from day one and never looked back. Whatever you choose, your baby will be fine—it's more about you and what feels right.

If you're ready for a little more rest, push yourself a bit out of your comfort zone and just try a few nights with your baby in another room. If you're undecided, start by moving the crib farther across the room as a first step. If your options are limited, you can even try moving the crib to a bathroom or walk-in closet—this is something we do with our second child when we're on vacation or staying with relatives, rather than bunking with her noisy self. Once you adjust, you might even find you have much better quality time with him upon waking.

[*No.*] 49 | BABY TOYS
are OVERRATED

Someday, your child will have *to have a Spider-Man web-thrower, a Disney Princess karaoke machine, or the latest scooter.* Save your money for that day. Do *not* spend it on a bunch of baby toys. Want to know what our second baby enjoyed playing with most yesterday? A pack of panty liners. The squishiness of the soft plastic packaging, the crinkling sound the paper made, the fact she could easily grip it in one hand and then fling it across the bathroom floor, scampering after it—what she decided was appealing on the bathroom shelf might've taken months of research at the toy store.

Other favorite playthings have included an empty Vaseline jar, a roll of masking tape, a shoe box with a hinged lid, a nail brush, and any DVD case that she could get her hands on. Meanwhile, the expensive European rattle gathers dust under the couch. Just goes to show you, "baby toys" are everywhere—so second-time parents have learned not to buy them.

Here are some of our favorites that you likely already own. If not, a few bucks in a housewares section and you're all set. Added bonus: you won't worry if you lose them!

▶ Plastic measuring spoons joined by a ring (these are also easy to attach to car seats, swings, and strollers)

▶ Plastic measuring cups and funnels (great in the tub too)

▶ Tupperware containers with lids (or any washed recyclable plastic containers, like those for yogurt or salsa)

▶ Plastic kitchen timers, egg timers, and board-game sand timers

SECOND-TIMER TIP

Save your outdated versions of personal electronics starting when you are pregnant. Amazingly, babies often turn up their noses at toy versions of phones, cameras, or remotes, but they'll usually fall for last year's models!

SECOND-TIMER TIP

Don't throw away your old wallet when you buy a new one. Stock it with your expired driver's license, outdated membership cards, and other useless cards and it will seem like the real deal to your baby or toddler. Keep it in the car to hand back during fussy drives or by your changing station for a child who is wild at diaper time.

{ SECOND-TIMER TIP

*Put masking tape or duct tape over
the speakers of noisy electronic toys if they
don't have a volume control.* }

- Metal mixing bowls (particularly entrancing on a hard kitchen floor)
- Empty boxes of all sizes
- Laundry baskets
- Shopping bags filled with tissue paper
- Sheer scarves
- Magazines and catalogs
- Your cell phone, sunglasses, keys, wallet, digital camera, and remote controls

*"Instead of buying one of those
expensive black-and-white baby mobiles that
are supposed to stimulate newborns,
I just drew patterns on white paper with a
Sharpie. Then for another version, I took strips
of black and white construction paper
and wove them into a waffle pattern. I taped
these next to the changing table and
around the house where he could see them—
he loved them! And he didn't care
if they weren't perfect."*

—TARA, MOM OF TWO, AGES 3 & 1

[*No.*] 50 | CHILDPROOF WHEN
the BABY is MOBILE

Second-time parents all have a familiar refrain on this topic: don't go overboard with the childproofing, and, honestly, don't start worrying about it as soon as you bring the baby home from the hospital (or when you're still pregnant!). Childproofing *is* important, but a first-timer's timeline tends to skew way too early—and covering all your outlets before baby is sitting up will only drive the grown-ups crazy. Of course, if it's one of those things that's keeping you up at night as a new parent, it's okay to do it sooner than necessary. But if you're feeling sleep-deprived and stressed, put this on the mental calendar for later. You have enough to do around the house already. Remember, your baby won't be mobile until six months at the earliest, and he won't be walking until around a year. Childproofing can be done in a day if necessary—and many a parent has done it!

> *"The second time, we decided to limit the number of rooms that we'd babyproof, instead of trying to make the entire house child-safe. The twins were happy with their space, and we love gates!"*
>
> —LINDSAY, MOM OF THREE, AGES 5, 2 & 2

[*No.*] 51 | YOU CAN ACCOMPLISH THINGS
WHILE BABY is AWAKE

All first-time parents feel like they have no time. They can't manage to wash a dish, much less think about dinner. Yet second-time parents often run a busy household—including chores, meals, carpooling, and taking care of a toddler—during this same baby stage. This is because they've learned that you *can* use your baby's waking hours to get things done.

First-timers tend to stay by baby's side constantly while she's awake and save all the household chores for naptime. Funnily enough, second-timers often do the opposite—saving chores for when the kids are awake, and using naptime for things they cannot possibly do with two active children, like reading a book on the couch, talking on the phone, checking e-mail, or shopping online.

If you work outside the home, you might feel an even bigger sense of guilt about even cleaning up the breakfast dishes or paying bills when the baby is awake, because every shared moment feels precious. And time with your baby *is* precious. But life does need to go on. It honestly doesn't hurt for your baby to learn early on that your every moment cannot be solely devoted to her entertainment, that you are all part of a larger family and household that needs care.

Taking your baby on errands, having her "help" you around the house, and giving her safe household objects (plasticware, wooden spoons) while she watches you cook are important life lessons—for both of you. And, of course, you can make funny faces, sing silly songs, tell her stories about what you're doing, and otherwise interact with your baby while doing all sorts of productive things. By the second child, parents learn that there are lots of ways to turn almost any task into an activity for baby—and the best use for naptime is rest.

Have a bunch of things to do and your baby is not content to play independently? Here are some ideas on how to involve her:

- Put baby in your carrier of choice—sling, backpack, BabyBjörn—while putting away groceries or laundry, doing dishes, tidying up, or even vacuuming (as long as your back is okay).

- Babies love laundry. They all enjoy the sensation of a clean sheet floating above their head like a parachute, playing peekaboo with a towel, tipping things out of the basket, or pulling up on it. Put your infant in the middle of the living room floor and enjoy the folding and sorting together.

▸ Place her in the infant seat or high chair with an assortment of measuring spoons and other clattering kitchen utensils while you make dinner, load the dishwasher, or just sit and have coffee and "chat" with her.

▸ Create a low cupboard that's full of baby-safe items like Tupperware and aluminum mixing bowls. Let your baby go crazy while you cook, put away groceries, or do any kitchen tasks.

▸ Keep a plastic bin of bath toys on your bathroom floor or in a low drawer. Your empty, clean moisturizer jars or shampoo bottles (without small caps) might be especially fascinating. Let baby play while you freshen up or blow-dry your hair.

▸ Grocery stores, drug stores, the post office, and other places where you're running errands are great eye-opening experiences for babies. If you find she gets restless in the car seat or stroller, bring along a baby carrier. Talk to her about what you're buying—colors, shapes, smells—and stop to chat with friendly people.

[No.] 52 | YOU DON'T HAVE TO BATHE
BABY EVERY NIGHT

Ask any second-time mom when her baby last had a bath and the answer will likely be, "Um . . . Tuesday?" Not only is it *not* a nightly occurrence by any stretch, the new sibling's "bath" is likely a sponge-down on the changing table or perhaps a below-the-waist dunk in the sink. First-timers, on the other hand, might feel it's best to bathe their child nightly, complete with a multitude of toys, a special hooded towel, and a variety of parent-provided songs and entertainment like a vaude-ville floor show. If an extravagant bath becomes a vital part of the bed-time routine, you may worry that baby won't sleep without it.

Lots of babies love their bath, and when time and energy permit, why not do it? But it's simply not necessary daily. "How dirty do babies get, anyway?" asks a mom of two active boys. "Bathe 'em every other day—at most. It's a production and gets to be a bigger production as they get older. Keeping it less frequent means they don't come to expect it as part of going to bed. Plus, it keeps their skin from getting too dry, saves your back, and keeps you from having to do more laundry or straighten up the bathroom yet again."

Newborn bathing can seem especially daunting—they just seem so frag-ile, and none of the infant tubs or your sinks seems exactly right. They get cold, you worry about them slipping around in the water, and, some-how, it all makes a huge mess. So take a cue from second-timers and get out a soft washcloth and a cozy towel for a sponge bath on your bed, changing table, or bathroom rug. (And remember, new babies need little or no baby wash or shampoo—pediatricians usually advise just plain clean water on that sensitive skin. One less thing to buy!)

YOU DON'T HAVE
TO CONSTANTLY

INTERACT *with your* BABY

This morning, while trying to get our older daughter ready for school, we glanced into the bathroom and saw our eight-month-old concentrating very hard on something. She was taking a lid on and off a toy pail, figuring out how it worked, noticing how it fit one way but not the other. It made us stop for a moment and wonder, "Did we ever catch our first child doing that, at that age, on her own?" The truth is, she probably never had the chance—one or both of us would most likely have been sitting right there with her, directing the activity.

Recently, a first-time mom friend of ours confessed, "I watch TV when I'm hanging out with my newborn. Is that terrible?" Another new mom admits to feeling guilty for checking her BlackBerry with one hand while cradling her dozing baby with the other. The truth is, as much as you imagine spending countless hours gazing meaningfully at your new baby, second-time moms know that you simply can't do that all day (and here's a little secret: you might actually get bored sometimes!). Plus, they don't need you to. Babies need lots of love and attention, of course, but they can also blossom when left to their own devices now and then.

SECOND-TIMER TIP

As your child grows, allow him to make some connections himself—swatting the toys above his play mat, trying to get that ball in the bowl over and over again, or rattling the drawer pulls—rather than showing him.

It's truly okay to let your baby have a little alone time—second children get a whole lot of it, and they turn out just fine. In fact, it could be the reason they tend to seem more independent and adaptable. So if your child is contentedly playing with a toy, staring at the ceiling fan, or just busy discovering his feet, you can let him be. While he's at it, you are allowed to flip through a magazine, refill your coffee, or make a personal phone call.

A little personal space is good for all children: babies, toddlers, and preschoolers (and down the road, teenagers!). It's also good for parents. Someday, you'll have to pull away from your baby a little out of necessity—whether that's to accommodate another child, to return to work, or just to keep up with life as it progresses. If your baby understands that you are there for him when he needs you, and that you are close by even when you're not actively interacting with him, this will be easier for both of you to accept as perfectly okay.

[No.] 54 | YOU DON'T HAVE TO SUBJECT YOURSELF to kids' MUSIC

"Don't get suckered into so-called kids' music for your little ones," advises a dad of three. "Listening to the Little People or Alvin and the Chipmunks may feel like a slow form of torture. They are never too young to learn to appreciate the beauty of other kinds of music."

With our first child, we owned a stack of baby-oriented CDs featuring classic lullabies, world music, Mozart for babies, and even everyday sounds meant to quell crying. We tried them all and always had them playing any time the baby was awake, either at home or in the car. We danced and rocked her to them for every nap and bedtime. We even took them with us when we traveled. They were the background music of our new life as parents, and they drove us absolutely crazy. We even heard Kermit warbling "Rainbow Connection" in our sleep.

We have no idea where those CDs are now. Our second baby listens to the music of the house, whether that's my older child's newfound love of '80s dance hits or our grown-up favorites. Car trips now mean car music, the kind we listened to before parenthood—'80s, Motown, alternative rock. And bedtime? Sure, we still hum a round or two of "Twinkle, Twinkle Little Star" or "Mr. Sandman" before dropping number two in her crib, but as opposed to number one's routine of seven or eight tracks of singing animals, that's all she expects. And she's happy with it.

> *"Start them early on all kinds of music, and you'll enjoy car trips a lot more for years to come. Currently, the most frequent request from my six-year-old on our commute to school is AC/DC's 'For Those About to Rock (We Salute You).' For my youngest, it's 'Eye of the Tiger' by Survivor. Getting to pick the first song on the way to school is also pure motivation for them getting ready in the morning."*
>
> —NEVILLE, DAD OF THREE, AGES 6, 4 & 2

We remember when our pediatrician suggested playing some of our own music—loudly—to combat witching hour with our first baby. We blasted the Canadian-Celtic band Great Big Sea and had a family sing-along, and it soothed her (and us) better than anything we'd ever tried. That was the beginning of the end of "baby music" in our house. Interestingly, our second baby didn't really suffer from a witching hour in the same way, perhaps because around 6 P.M. we're all busy getting the family's dinner ready and she is on the floor, wiggling happily to the Black Eyed Peas.

See also, "The 'Witching Hour' Is Not a Myth" (pg. 56).

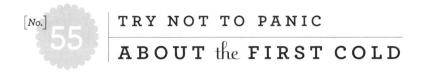

TRY NOT TO PANIC
ABOUT *the* FIRST COLD

A feeling of utter helplessness often accompanies your first baby's first illness, even if it's just the sniffles. You might find yourself sleeping next to her crib, worrying about every labored breath, and taking her temperature every waking hour. While you should certainly check in with your pediatrician or nurse helpline if you have any concerns about an infant's health, if it really is just a cold, there is not much you can do but wait it out. One thing second-time parents know is that they will get through it, and it *always* sounds worse than it is. Alas, doctors do not recommend any cold medicine for young children. The best remedies are the same as for an adult—plenty of rest and lots of liquids for the patient. Here are a few things you can do (but first check with your doctor concerning issues particular to your child):

▶ **ELEVATE ONE SIDE OF THE CRIB SLIGHTLY.** Put a paperback book under the head end of the crib, or place a towel between the crib mattress and springs, to help with postnasal drip.

▶ **TRY TO IGNORE THE MUCUS (AVOID CONSTANT WIPING).** As disgusting as it may be to see snot running out of your baby's nose all day, it's better out than in. Keep soft cloths around to wipe when you can't stand it anymore.

▶ **ASK YOUR DOCTOR ABOUT USING A BULB SYRINGE/SALINE FLUSH.** Some doctors advise flushing your baby's nose with over-the-counter saline and then removing it with a bulb syringe (especially if the congestion is preventing nursing); others say it does nothing but irritate the already-inflamed nasal cavity.

▶ **ASK YOUR DOCTOR ABOUT USING A HUMIDIFIER OR COOL-MIST VAPORIZER.** Again, some doctors recommend these (and some parents swear by using them all winter), while other doctors say they're nothing but a breeding ground for bacteria. Another way to get this effect is to sit with your baby in a warm, steamy bathroom with the shower running.

> *"I remember to be thankful every day*
> *that my girls are healthy, in the big sense.*
> *I don't sweat the small stuff with Lucy. If*
> *she has a cold, so be it. We don't rush to the*
> *doctor with every runny nose."*
>
> —JANE, MOM OF THREE, AGES 10, 6 & 1

Of course, second-time parents are usually able to take minor illnesses in stride, not only because they know everything's okay, but because older siblings still have to get to school or activities and baby's got to come along for the ride. It's rare that an experienced parent will cancel a date night or stay home from work because a baby has a cough. But the first time *your* baby gets sick—even a little—it's a parenting milestone. You worry. So if you find it difficult to leave your baby's side and you don't have to, don't. Coddle her. Cancel your plans. Stay home. Do what feels right.

[*No.*] 56 | ## YOU DON'T HAVE TO RUSH HOME
to **PUT YOUR BABY** to **BED**

We have always believed in having our kids nap at home, in their own cribs, when possible. It is what works best for us. But we have come to realize with our second child that naptime doesn't have to totally rule our day—which is key when you have an older child who doesn't nap anymore and everyone can't come to a screeching halt for baby's snooze. If your baby is still a newborn, chances are you already have a favorite sleeping spot with you, wherever you go: his stroller or infant car seat. It's okay to let him sleep there when you're out and about.

When your baby is more than six months old, though, he may be falling into a nap schedule and prefer to sleep in a crib. But that doesn't mean you have to hightail it home when the clock strikes two. If you'd like to spend the day with friends or relatives and no crib is available, just bring along a Pack 'n Play and a favorite blanket or toy, and put him down there. What's the worst that can happen? Commit to trying it more than once, and you might open up a whole lot more freedom for yourself. If taking the portable crib seems too cumbersome, your baby carrier might be another option—many babies nap comfortably in a wrap or a sling until well past one year—or use the car seat. Some babies even sleep quite comfortably on a blanket or futon on the floor, if they've gotten used to it.

The same goes for bedtime. We like to have our baby fall asleep on time and at home, but we make exceptions. When we took our baby on a trip at around four months, we didn't want to have to leave our friends' house at 7:30 P.M. and sit at our hotel. Instead, we put her down at their house and stayed to visit until midnight, then gently woke her to take her home. Three nights out of four, we transferred her successfully to the car seat and then to the hotel crib without a peep. The fourth night, she protested and needed some rocking and nursing to go down again—but still, not bad odds, and a much more enjoyable trip for us.

[*No.*] 57 | YOU CAN LEAVE YOUR BABY
with OTHER PEOPLE

What do second-timers say about babysitters? "If anyone— *anyone!*—within reason offers to babysit, say yes before she changes her mind!" That's easy to say if you're a seasoned parent of two or three kids of varying ages and you've done it a thousand times. But the first few times of leaving a young baby are tough for everyone—particularly new moms. So why do it? Well, if you *ever* want to spend time away from your child—and you will—young babyhood is a great time to get her used to being cared for by other trusted people. It's an important part of any child's development, and waiting until after separation anxiety sets in (usually around nine months) can make the adjustment more difficult. In contrast, at around three months, a parent out of sight is pretty much out of mind, making it easier on both caregiver and child.

Still, even if you know this intellectually, how can you leave such a helpless little being with anyone else? What if she wonders where you are? And what might you miss? Second-timers question these issues a lot less, if at all; they know that not only will she be fine away from her parents, but the break will be good for everyone. Remind yourself of an inarguable truth: there are plenty more days of togetherness to come—your whole life, in fact!

To get past the initial hurdle, a good rule of thumb is to start with short outings and stay nearby, so you know you can be home quickly. Assure your caregiver that it's okay to contact you if you're needed. (In this age of cell phones, it may help to think of your babysitter as a long-distance monitor.) But chances are everything will go beautifully and you'll be pleasantly surprised—and maybe a tiny bit hurt—to see a perfectly happy baby upon your return.

Only you can decide your comfort level with the concept of babysitters, but here are some tips to ease you into it:

▶ Pick a time of day or night that feels most comfortable to you, based on your baby's loose schedule. Even though she will likely be perfectly fine being put to bed by someone else (young babies don't have the emotional attachment to bedtime that we do), choose a daytime outing if that feels better.

▶ If your baby has a consistent and relatively early bedtime, consider going out after she's in bed (if you have the energy). Even though this technique doesn't get your baby accustomed to other caregivers, it might bolster your confidence in leaving the house. This is a perfect one to try when the grandparents are visiting.

If you feel more comfortable leaving your baby with family members or friends who are parents, reach out to them first. Admit you're feeling nervous. Stay in your neighborhood and do something low-key: take a walk, have lunch, or see a matinee. Know that you can be home in a few minutes if needed.

If you're nursing exclusively, you may only have two hours (or less) of freedom from your baby. Don't let that stop you. Squeeze in a stroll, quick meal, or coffee and dessert with your partner between baby's nursing sessions.

When you're ready to look further afield for sitters, talk to other parents for referrals or use a reputable service. Colleges offering childhood development programs are another great resource.

See also, "Let Your Partner Do Things His Way" (pg. 72) and "Find a Support System—Early" (pg. 37).

[No.]
58

YOU AND YOUR PARTNER WILL
ARGUE—POSSIBLY A LOT

When you and your partner first bring home your little bundle of joy, the sheer emotion of the experience is surreal, and the day-to-day pressures seem to melt away while gazing at your beautiful creation. You are a family now. Everything is perfect. You are so lucky. Nothing else matters. At first. Second-time parents know that, inevitably, the reality of being a parent sets in, and when it does, it can be fast and furious. Who else to take it out on but your parenting partner?

Maternity/paternity leave—if you have it—quickly disappears, and even the most prepared couples find themselves with an increase in the amount that needs to get done and a decrease in time or energy to do it. And this isn't just for the families with both parents returning to work; in fact, this stress can be magnified when one parent assumes the role of the primary caregiver, because resentment can build on both sides. Given how much energy you are putting into your new child and how your sleep is being affected, it's normal that fuses will be a bit shorter and little annoyances once easily brushed aside can grow into larger issues. This can even lead to what we like to call the "Un-winnable Argument" that begins with a seemingly straightforward question: *Who is working harder?*

When disagreements, arguments, or even full-blown fights begin to rear up, it will help to remember that you are a team. Sure, there will be moments when you think your spouse is doing everything wrong or that he or she is simply not doing enough. This might be due to displaced anger or blame about the tasks at hand; it might be fear causing you to stress out; it might simply be that your partner is the only other adult in your world and you have to unleash this emotion on someone. Now, do you always have the right to lash out because of all of this? Well, no.

The irony here is that this is one of the first big lessons you will soon be teaching your toddler: it's okay to have these kinds of feelings, but it isn't okay to act out against others because of them. Second-time parents have discovered that the path to resolution always seems to come back to that one tried-and-true thing: communication. A constant stream of communication with your partner can certainly take some of the fizz out of the bottle; it's no secret that even a feeling of complete frustration and anger can seem more manageable when taken out of your head and put into context with your mate. Even when you're not totally feeling it, try to sympathize. Saying "I understand" and "I'm sorry" and "thank you" goes a long way toward diffusing any situation.

Let your partner vent when he or she needs to, and resist the urge to one-up each other ("You think *your* day was hard?"). This is not a contest. Encourage each other to take breaks—not only from the baby, but from each other. Have a solo workout, an outing to a coffee shop with the paper, or even a walk around the block. Fresh air, even just for a moment, does wonders.

> *"One thing I learned by the second child was to say 'thank you' to my husband now and then. With our first, I stayed home, and I was so wrapped up in how hard my job was that I kind of forgot he was working at all. Now I try to remember to thank him for little things, like dealing with his commute without complaining about it, or picking up dinner or a gallon of milk on his way home."*
>
> —ANNA, MOM OF TWO, AGES 5 & 3

It's important to note that there are times when even the best attempts at communication and understanding can fail. Conditions such as postpartum depression can influence just how much you as a new family can accomplish. If you're concerned this is the case for you, it's no time to just grin and bear it. If you are feeling consistently overwhelmed and overcome by your situation, the bravest—and smartest—thing you can do is move quickly to get your family the help it needs. Ask your doctor for the name of a couples' or personal counselor. Get a mutually respected family member to help with perspective. Talk to your parents' group or other parents you admire for advice. The key is to find the common ground needed to move on from this point and refocus—together—on the joy that being a new family can bring.

See also, "It Might Feel as If You and Your Partner Live on Separate Planets" (pg. 122).

[No.] 59 | GO AHEAD
and COMPLAIN

Do you feel like a failure if you admit your baby is driving you bonkers? Are you silently aggravated by everything your partner does? Do your conversations with other new parents feel false because everyone is just saying how hunky-dory it is? Who knows why, but first-time parents are often hesitant to complain—especially to anyone outside their closest friends or family. They keep their cards close to their vests, fretting that their complaining might be misconstrued, that their frustration might be equated with poor parenting. Meanwhile, second-time parents do nothing but talk about how out-of-control their households feel and how many times they consider sending their kids to boarding school. They complain to absolutely anyone who will listen; in fact, they sometimes try to out-complain each other ("You think that's bad? Guess what my monsters did yesterday . . . I want to throttle them both!").

Think about it: you probably complained about your job all the time before you had a baby, so why is it suddenly unseemly to complain about your new job—the most stressful one of all—parenthood? You don't have to go all the way and air your dirty laundry to everyone you encounter, but you do have to complain. Yes, *have* to. You have to admit that you're overwhelmed, that your baby is being a pain, that you're mad at your partner, that you sometimes wish for "the old days" with every fiber of your being. You have to admit these things and then realize, at the end of the day, that you are still a good parent and that your partner and your baby still love you.

See, the walls don't come tumbling down because you admit you feel inept, or ambivalent, or mad, or crazy. Instead, you will get it off your chest and, like most problems that seem darkest when we keep them hidden, things will seem more manageable once you give them a name and let them out into the light. So go ahead, complain about your baby!

Vent and grumble and whine and moan—and then let it go. As experienced parents know, there will be something new to commiserate about tomorrow.

See also, "Find a Support System—Early" (pg. 37).

[No.] 60 | YOU CAN (AND SHOULD) EXERCISE

A healthy dose of exercise is good for the spirit as well as the body. If it seems insurmountable in the first few months after baby is born, you're not alone. But second-time parents have figured out ways to work it in, because keeping up your strength and energy gets even more important from here on out. Here are some ideas to ease into it:

▶ **FIND A POSTNATAL CLASS.** Many yoga studios and gyms offer classes specifically for new moms—and babies are welcome. The warm room and mellow vibe tend to keep them calm and sleepy.

▶ **RENT AN EXERCISE VIDEO.** Yoga and Pilates are easy to do in your living room while baby is sleeping or on his play mat. Rent a few DVDs from the library if you're not sure what to try first. Invite a friend to join you and you'll be more likely to actually do the moves, rather than nap.

TRY THE DROP-OFF DAYCARE AT YOUR HEALTH CLUB. It will seem scary at first, but when your baby is still in the first sleepy months, leaving him with a licensed provider while you do an hour of cardio will work out great. And if you and your child come to find this both fun and familiar, you have years of stress-free exercise plus leisurely showers and steams in your future.

CHECK INTO NEIGHBORHOOD AND COMMUNITY CENTER CLASSES. Some offer basic aerobics and other classes with the option of using their childcare provider in the playroom for a nominal fee.

SWAP TIME WITH ANOTHER PARENT. If you have a trusted friend with a baby, alternate days at each other's houses and let one person go exercise while the other provides attentive, in-home childcare for an hour. The babies will enjoy looking at each other and, later, playing together in a familiar space.

SWAP TIME WITH YOUR SPOUSE. You've both probably put exercise on the back burner. Schedule one evening or weekend day per week when each of you gets guilt-free workout time.

WALK (OR RUN) EVERYWHERE. Invest in a good rain cover for your stroller and outdoor gear for yourself, and go out in any weather. Run errands (pushing a stroller full of groceries is a great workout), talk on the phone, bring along a friend, or do it together as a family . . . and get your exercise at the same time.

INCORPORATE BABY INTO YOUR WORKOUT. As your baby gets bigger and stronger, so can you. There's something to be said for lying on your back and bench-pressing the little one. Not only will you generate some excellent giggles, you might just generate a little muscle too!

IT'S OKAY FOR YOU AND YOUR BABY TO
"DO NOTHING" *all* DAY

Look at all those parents running while pushing their babies in jogging strollers, complete with dogs and cell phones, taking their little ones to classes, going on hikes, hitting all the kids' concerts, arranging playdates, even for precrawlers!

There are new parents who like their days chock-full, traveling to faraway parks or birthday parties, visiting museums and community centers, checking out various cultural events. But if you just don't have the energy or inclination, you are *not* short-changing your baby. Frankly, what young babies seem to crave most is time in familiar surroundings with familiar people doing familiar things. It is perfectly reasonable to spend most of the newborn year hanging out at home, venturing out to a nearby park or library, going on simple errands, and people-watching or visiting within your neighborhood. (That's all the "socialization" a baby of this age needs, and don't let anyone tell you otherwise.) All of these things are a great education for a baby. And you will likely find that when you do bundle her up and make the effort to go to the aquarium or the zoo, what fascinates her most are the pigeons, squirrels, and other little kids that she could've seen for free on your own street.

It's important right now to take it easy on yourselves. You're both new at this, and there is no need to push yourself; you both deserve to be comforted and comfortable. If you don't feel like doing something—even if several of your new-parent friends are doing it—then don't. Ask any parent who has hit the one-year mark, and he or she will likely say that the most magical moments they had with their baby took place on the living room floor, not at the science center or the children's museum.

You and your child will have your whole lives together to check out that new sculpture exhibit across town. The toddler years are right around the corner, and by then you'll have a sense what she (and you) will enjoy and benefit from most. By the time she's walking, you'll have some favorite activities that arise naturally—story time at a local bookstore, meeting friends at a park, or making chalk drawings on your driveway—and you'll have found your ideal pace too.

Until then, if today feels like a stay-home-in-our-pajamas sort of day, make it one.

See also, "Your Baby Does Not Need Classes" (pg. 128).

[No.] 62 | YOU WILL GET
ANGRY at YOUR BABY

As an excited new parent, the last thing on your mind is the notion that you could get angry at your baby. But, as a friend confessed recently, "You know how before you have one, you can't believe anyone could ever shake their baby? Then you have one, and the astonishing thing is that anyone manages *not* do it." It's hard to even repeat that, but in the moment it can feel that way. This type of anger is such a surprise among new parents that it often blindsides them. It is also one of the aspects of parenthood that seems the least talked about, especially for first-timers—there is a stigma associated with the mere notion that one could get mad at a baby. What kind of parent could do that? Does it mean you are not fit to be one? Second-timers not only know that they can and will get mad at their child, they are far more open to talking about it. And only through talking about it can parents defuse their anger—and the guilt and shame that tags along with it—and begin to find their way through it.

There really is no way to prepare a new parent for an inconsolable child, one who's succumbed to a full repertoire of soothing techniques yet refuses to cooperate and stop crying. Combine that with a parent's lack of sleep and all the related stresses of this new role and you get a recipe for the dark side of any personality. Some parents cry. Some yell. Some have terrible thoughts. Do not think you are abnormal for feeling the way you feel.

Just like they can bring out ultimate joys, babies can really get you where you live. And it's your job to be prepared. So take seriously those pamphlets that talk about shaking your baby, and make a vow to put your child down in a safe place and count to ten if you feel out of control. Getting frustrated? Take a break. If your partner is available, make the handoff. Go outside for a few moments, away from the noise. If you're on your own, put the baby safely down in the crib and take a breather; a baby has never been injured from howling in his crib. This pivotal moment, when you give yourself five minutes, is about getting you off the ledge and away from the swelling wave of emotion. Take it.

If you realize you might need more breaks from your baby during the day in order to keep your anger in check—especially if he is going through a particularly trying period—find some support, whether that's a hired babysitter, a neighbor whom you can call when you need a break, or a friend or relative who can stay with you for a while. If the added support isn't helping, talk to your doctor and look into classes or counseling that can help you manage your anger. Sound a bit scary? It can be, but not if you are aware of the possibility of these feelings and understand that it does not make you a bad parent.

See also, "Find a Support System—Early" (pg. 37).

[No.] 63 | PARENTHOOD CAN BE UNBELIEVABLY BORING

As a new parent, you will get bored. Bored . . . out . . . of . . . your . . . mind. Yes, even during that astounding and absorbing first year. As a first-timer, this may come as a surprise. You hear how parenthood will be busy, challenging, full of wonder, fulfilling, even aggravating . . . but *boring*? Oh, yes. You see, while everything your baby does for the first few weeks or months might earn your rapt attention and enthusiasm (and rightly so—truly there is nothing like those miraculous firsts, both big and small), life soldiers on. And on. And on. And as your baby nears one year, she'll begin the long (really long) stage of wanting to do the same thing over and over and over. Experienced parents know the hard truth: that while seeing her point at the kitties in *Goodnight Moon* or fill a cup with sand for the first time will amaze you, seeing it for the thousandth time that week can feel like watching paint dry. And that's not to mention the endless repetition of other dull parenting tasks, from washing bottles to making tiny mashed meals to changing diapers, day in and day out. It's relentless. But don't worry. Just when you find yourself bored out of your skull one afternoon, something new happens. She starts walking. Or talking. Or talking *back*. And suddenly, she's got your full attention again.

See also, "Everything—*Everything*—Is a Stage" (pg. 67).

[No.]
64

BECOME A MASTER OF TREATING
YOURSELF — QUICKLY

As a first-timer, you have a very important lesson to learn: how to relax, unwind, or recharge in a very short amount of time. If you find yourself with even thirty minutes to yourself before your baby wakes up, resist the urge to put in another load of laundry. Instead, grab that precious time and use it to treat yourself right—both you and your baby deserve it. What qualifies as a real treat varies with the individual, but think about some of these:

▶ Nap

▶ Enjoy a face mask, salt scrub, or bubble bath

- Have a drink on the deck
- Watch your favorite (previously recorded) TV show or sporting event
- Make an ice cream sundae or root beer float
- Bake some cookies using store-bought dough
- Make a phone call to a beloved friend
- Curl up with a fuzzy blanket and trashy magazine
- Read a good book that has nothing to do with child-rearing
- Do a little yoga or stretching
- Shoot baskets
- Write in a journal
- Blog
- Paint your toenails
- Garden
- Sketch
- Cook
- Play a video game
- Listen to your favorite music
- Order something beautiful for yourself or your home online
- Brew a fresh pot of coffee or tea and make cinnamon toast
- If you have the freedom, take a stroll . . . while carrying nothing

Have free time while with your partner? Try any of the above in tandem (yes, even the toenail painting!), as well as:

- Give reciprocal foot or shoulder rubs

- Play a board game
- Mix your favorite cocktails
- Toss a ball outside
- Snuggle
- Read to each other
- Have sex!

YOU AND YOUR PARTNER DON'T HAVE
to do EVERYTHING together

Repeat after us: take turns. Second-time parents have learned that the best thing about having only one child is that you and your partner get to do this. If you choose to have another baby, it will be a 1:1 parent-child ratio (or you'll be outnumbered by your kids!) from that moment on. Embrace your chance now to enjoy the guilt-free handoff.

> *"My wife and I take turns going out with our friends. We established early that every other Tuesday is my night with the guys, and every other Thursday is her girls' night. There's no babysitter expense or coordination, so it's easy to do more often than date nights."*
>
> —BRAD, DAD OF TWO, AGES 6 & 4

It's great if you're both hopelessly devoted to your first child. You should be. It's also great if you and your partner are both available, involved, and eager to participate in various key moments of the day, like feedings, playtime, bath time, and bedtime, so you can enjoy these rituals as a new little family. But here's the thing you quickly learn as a second-time parent: you don't *have* to do all of it together.

Our dear friends recently came for a visit, bringing their six-month-old. He was new to solid foods, and usually one parent was feeding him while the other made funny faces and encouraging noises until the meal was finished. Other friends came to stay with their one-year-old daughter. When it was bedtime, they both excused themselves to read her a story and put her to bed together. All of this seemed unusual to us until we reflected on our first year with our oldest. It seems so long ago now, but didn't we bathe her together every time, the two of us hanging over the edge of the tub to not miss a thing? Didn't we both go upstairs for all the little routines that came at bedtime, like pajamas, books, songs? It amazed us to think back to a time when we did all those tasks as a team, instead of alternating duties and letting one parent relax.

Now, don't get me wrong, there's certainly something wonderful about all that togetherness. And if one or both of you has demanding work schedules that mean those times are few, by all means, embrace them. But it's also important to learn that you *can* ask your spouse, *Can you do this one?* It's a natural progression that experienced parents do automatically. One parent does bath and pj's, and then hands off to the second parent for stories and bedtime. One parent feeds the baby while the other person preps a grown-up meal for later. One parent takes the baby to the birthday party while the other parent naps (or shops, or drinks, or watches TV).

Of course, when the second child arrives, no one really gets a break—so finding a happy rhythm of together time versus alone time is key now. For example, maybe you'll decide to alternate doing the whole bedtime routine each night, so that every other day, you get the luxury of some real alone time. (Tomorrow night will come soon enough, don't worry.) You can also alternate daytime responsibilities; you'll see a lot of dads out with their babies Saturday mornings, probably because Mom is on the morning shift during the workweek. Take turns when you want them, and you'll both feel more excited to be with the baby when it's your turn. Alas, first-time parents often feel a bit guilty about not being there every single minute. *What if I miss something adorable? What if my baby wonders where I am? What if he laughs for the first time over the sheer delight of tasting peas?* Let it go. Unless you really, *really* want to get up at 6 A.M. again this Saturday, let yourself have a much-deserved breather. And give your spouse the same dose of quiet time on Sunday. Remember that if you have a second child, you will have to divide and conquer all the time—one parent will be bathing number one while the other puts number two to bed; one will be spoon-feeding the baby while the other is cajoling the preschooler to swallow something green; one will be diapering the infant while the other will be endlessly sitting with the toddler on the potty. And free mornings will be a lot harder to come by. Take advantage of the fact that your family is still two-on-one.

[No.] 66 | **PERFECT NAPS EVERY DAY ARE NOT NECESSARY**
(at LEAST NOT for BABY)

My friend Jane had her third child when her first two were nine and five. "Oh, I remember those perfect naps," she says wistfully one day, while carting her newborn to her eldest daughter's riding lessons. "You know, when you let your baby sleep as long as he wants to? This baby *never* gets those."

Once your baby establishes a nap schedule, these hallowed times seem like an absolute necessity. Come hell or high water, that baby must nap, largely because you've planned your whole day (and your own free time) around it, and also because you may believe your baby's world will fall apart without it. Once you have more kids, you have no choice but to disrupt baby's naps for the needs of the older children: school pick-up and drop-off, doctors' appointments, activities, and playdates. And while no one wants to wake a sleeping baby, the little one will turn out okay anyway . . . and frankly, you might find the day is not a total loss after all. They are surprisingly resilient creatures.

So when your baby just seems to not want to nap one day—or gets disrupted for any number of reasons, including your own plans—don't fret. (And don't spend longer than a typical naptime trying to get him to change his mind!) Turn the light back on and grin and bear it. Remember that tomorrow is another day—one in which your baby probably will nap, and, hopefully, you will too!

[No.] 67 | YOUR SEX DRIVE
may HIT a DEAD-END

Once you're a new parent, you have a different sort of reaction when tabloids report that some celebrity mom's babies are only thirteen months apart. Rather than thinking, "Wow, that's going to be a lot of work," your first thought is likely, "You mean she had sex within four months of giving birth—and probably more than once?"

If you're like most first-time parents, you are probably surprised—and a little bit concerned—about how long it takes your sex drive to reappear. By your second, you'll know to expect it, making it less of an emotionally charged subject and one that's been navigated before. Sex after your first baby is tied up with a lot of issues; here are just a few:

▶ **PHYSICAL AND EMOTIONAL RECOVERY.** Both of you are dealing with new emotions and stresses on mind and body, as well as your sense of self. C-sections and vaginal births leave Mom's body with a lot of repair work, and there are both physical and emotional aspects to this recovery; it can be a long time before she feels like herself again. Breast-feeding sometimes exacerbates this process because she is still so physically tied to the baby. Dad may also find he views Mom and her body differently now that she has given birth, or he may worry about hurting her.

BODY IMAGE. Naturally, Mom is dealing with a roller coaster of weight and body changes. But it also can affect dads, many of whom gain weight during pregnancy and don't take it off.

HORMONES. Mom's hormones are on a roller coaster too—making her repeatedly weepy, angry, and either eager for sex or appalled by the idea.

ENERGY LEVEL. You're both exhausted, emotionally and physically drained, and have been dealing with disrupted sleep.

RESENTMENT. Does one spouse feel like he or she is doing more than his or her share? That is not an ideal recipe for the give-and-take of intimacy.

STRESS. All aspects of life are stressed after a baby. Both of you may be worried about not only your baby and the lifestyle changes that come with it, but also your finances, career, health, or even another pregnancy.

FEELING DISCONNECTED. "Our problem was that my husband needed to have sex to feel connected with me," explains one friend. "And I needed to feel connected in order to want sex." This is not uncommon. When one spouse goes back to work and the other spends all day with the baby, it can lead to mutual resentment and a feeling of isolation.

DISRUPTIONS. Here's one thing second-time parents can guarantee: no matter when or where you have sex for the first time after bringing baby home, you will hear her cry at some really inopportune moment.

Take a cue from second-time parents and talk about expectations, worries, and other things besides intercourse that might help you feel close. Does Mom crave more adult intimacy before she can even think about sex? Talk about what would help, from a regularly scheduled date night to a candlelit take-out dinner at home after baby is in bed. Does Dad want more sex than she does? Figure out a plan that seems acceptable to you both; perhaps a regular weekend naptime quickie (when both of you aren't exhausted) will keep you feeling connected but not over-extended in the sex department—and make sure the same effort is made to reestablish your intimacy on an emotional level.

Of course, finding nonsexual ways to express your affection—from complimenting each other to smooching on the couch—is a great way to stay close. The key is to keep a sense of humor and try not to be too disheartened, worried, or surprised when your formerly frisky love life seems MIA. Remember: it happens to everyone. And it will return. Like everything with your baby, this is a stage—and another one is always around the corner.

See also, "It Might Feel as If You and Your Partner Live on Separate Planets" (pg. 122).

[No.] 68 | BABIES CAN BE
PUT DOWN AWAKE

Every first-time parent seems to have this notion that babies should be rocked, and rocked, and rocked—then placed gently in their crib when fast asleep. And certainly, a beautiful feeling of satisfaction and accomplishment comes when you get your baby to drift into dreamland while in your arms. So feel free to do it, especially during the newborn weeks, when your baby (and you!) might crave a lot of physical comfort and contact to nod off, and when no routines have been established as far as sleeping and waking. But you simply can't do this indefinitely. Why? Because as baby becomes more aware, you want him to learn to soothe himself and be comfortable falling asleep on his own. After all, you can't always be there until he falls fast asleep, can you?

A friend of ours has a two-and-a-half-year-old who still has to be rocked to sleep at both naptime and bedtime. "His grandparents used to take care of him a lot during the day, and they wanted to get him sound asleep before putting him down for nap," she says. "It was hard to deprive them of that. But now, I need him to nap—and he won't go down any other way except by endless rocking." She realizes she's now reinforcing the behavior she wants to stop, but she feels stuck because the pattern is so ingrained. She's now expecting her second baby. Do you think she'll have this kind of time to spend getting her toddler to sleep when she's also juggling an infant? Not likely. "It will be a rude awakening," she admits.

In a family of two, three, or more kids, parents learn quickly when a fussy baby truly needs attention; when he doesn't, he's expected to soothe himself. There's simply no way to spend forty-five minutes getting a baby off to sleep when you have other young, demanding children who are awake. But here's the thing that all second-time parents have learned: you don't have to spend forty-five minutes if you don't want to. If you start early on, you might only have to spend fifteen, or even five, minutes, if that's what you would like. You might ease back from singing ten songs, for example, and try singing two and let a CD play the rest. Or you might try gently jiggling or stroking him while he's in the crib rather than picking him up.

Now, bedtime will not come this easily for all families. If you have a restless or colicky baby, you may have more challenges with putting him down awake. Talk to your pediatrician or other moms for ideas on weaning him from your presence gradually. There are a multitude of "sleep system" books on the marketplace offering different techniques, and it is best if someone can help guide you to one that worked for their family, although babies are (infuriatingly) unique.

Just remember, no matter if the bedtime process is relatively easy or excruciatingly difficult for your family, like so many things the first year, your baby finding his way to sleep is a life skill he *must* learn. So try not to feel guilty about not getting him completely sound asleep before you leave the room. You are actually doing him a service. Anything you can do to gently guide him to independence and self-reliance is not only part of your job, it's the essence of good parenting.

See also, "Endeavor to Keep It Simple" (pg. 63) and "Discipline Is Not a Four-Letter Word" (pg. 151).

[No.]
69

EARPLUGS
are YOUR FRIEND

Ask any second-time parent: you have got to embrace earplugs. Don't be shy about it. We buy these in bulk and have them in our bedroom, bathroom, guest room, and the glove box of our car. Why? Children are *loud*. When they are babies, they are loud unintentionally, and when they get older, they are loud on purpose. Obviously, you won't use earplugs when you're in charge of your sleeping infant or driving a car. But any time you're not in charge of your baby, for a few minutes or a few hours, you'll find it's much easier to relax if you can't hear the full decibel level of every cry, or, later, even every laugh or squeal. So put them in and get into bed or the tub, pronto.

Here are a few scenarios during which you will want to use earplugs:

▹ When your mother comes to visit and offers to take the midnight shift; tell her to nudge you when it's your turn to feed the baby

▹ When your spouse is doing the early morning shift on the weekend or tells you to go nap

- When anyone else is in charge for a period of time

- During witching hour or any other inconsolable periods

- To offer to overnight guests

- When your baby is screaming in the car and you're the passenger (there is nothing louder and more anxiety-producing than a crying infant in the car when you are unable to do anything to help)

- When your baby has taken to screeching (happily or otherwise) every time she's in the high chair

- When you sleep in the same room with your baby, whether due to house-guests, or a hotel stay, or just because that's where she is right now.

Don't worry, earplugs are not impenetrable. You will hear cries (and even moans and grunts) just fine through them. But they *can* at least take the edge off.

[No.] 70 "DINING OUT" DOESN'T HAVE TO MEAN "DISASTER"

New parents tend to be overly nervous about taking their baby to a restaurant. They pray he'll sleep and they worry about every little peep. We understand: even at a family-friendly café, one of us would take our first baby for a walk around the block if she started to fuss in the slightest. We don't worry so much anymore, but we've also learned a few tricks to make it go more smoothly.

- **PICK THE RIGHT PLACE.** Naturally, don't take your baby to a place where children would be unwelcome. If you're meeting others, don't hesitate to suggest an alternate venue if it will be a better experience for all. When you arrive, ask for a table in the back or wherever you'll be most comfortable.

PLAN FOR A GOOD TIME OF DAY. Lunch is often better than dinner, and restaurants are usually more relaxed then too.

NURSE YOUR BABY BEFOREHAND. Try to nurse or give your baby his bottle either before you go to the restaurant or as soon as you sit down.

BRING SOME FOOD. If he's eating solids, bring a few finger foods—especially things that will take him a while to eat, like a frozen whole-wheat bagel or teething biscuit. If you want to order something for your baby, do it as soon as you're seated, and don't be shy to ask for things not specifically on the menu (sliced avocado or banana, a single piece of toast or cheese). Your server wants your baby to be happy too, so it's in his or her best interest to accommodate you.

MAKE BABY SECURE. Don't spend the meal worrying about his safety. If he's sitting up but not really solid in those wooden restaurant highchairs, roll up your coat or ask for a couple of bar towels to tuck around him. Or bring a clip-on seat.

> *"If food falls on the floor now,*
> *I brush it off and put it back on my son's plate.*
> *Although I do draw the line at food falling*
> *too close to the cats' litter box."*
> —JENNIFER, MOM OF TWO, AGES 3 & 2

TRY THE UNEXPECTED. Keep in mind that family-friendly does not have to mean fast food. For example, we love sushi restaurants with our kids: babies can enjoy tofu, spoonfuls of miso soup, crab meat, cooked fish, dumplings, noodles, and avocado—plus, we usually find speedy service and a willingness to bring things out in stages. Try a restaurant that both the adults and baby can enjoy, and you might find a new family favorite.

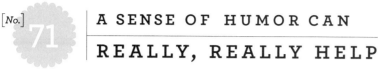

A SENSE OF HUMOR CAN
REALLY, REALLY HELP

The first time around, it's hard to find the humor in all the ridic-ulousness of parenthood: being peed on, having Mom's breasts leak in the middle of a date night, going to work with spit-up down your back. By the second time, these things are easier to laugh about ... and then let go of.

How that's accomplished is a matter of self-discovery, since not all cou-ples find the same element of humor in the same situations. But we'd be willing to bet that one of you has an inner clown that can be summoned at the most dire of moments. If that's you, bring it on and see how it can change the mood of a tense situation. If that's your spouse, find the inner generosity to let him or her try it out and win you over. And don't get caught in the trap of new-parent defensiveness, whereby you refuse to be amused about anything involving your baby, your body, or your par-enting. Instead of automatically responding with *What's so funny about that?*, attempt what second-timers endeavor to do: look at the bigger picture and let yourself be amused.

You also have to embrace your goofy side when it comes to interacting with your baby. Silly humor will lighten any mood, for both of you, and get you through some moments that would otherwise require gritted teeth and whiskey. If slapstick comedy is not normally your thing, it might take some coaxing. You've got to let all former vestiges of cool float away. You've got to find the silliness in a kitchen splattered with mashed peas and an infant screeching like a baby condor when your single friends come to the door. You've got to sing a dopey song and make a pack of baby wipes dance in the grocery line, without a speck of self-consciousness. You've *got* to. Any second-time parent will tell you: until you can warble an appealingly outrageous rhyme about a poopy diaper, complete with hand movements, you are not truly a parent. (The day is coming. Be ready.)

This skill will also serve you well as your baby enters toddlerhood, when being silly instead of strict during tense situations can help you navigate all sorts of daily obstacles, from struggling to get her into her car seat to trying to get her to swallow something other than macaroni. Make it funny, make it a game, let her see your silly side, and the desire to butt heads with you might disappear, at least for a moment. Not to mention the good lesson you're giving her about not sweating the small stuff.

Nearly every second-time parent we talked to, no matter what else he or she had to share, had one similar piece of advice: don't take everything so seriously. Laugh when you can, even if it's not until days later. Always remind yourself: your baby isn't doing this to you on purpose. You've got that coming later on. So learning to chuckle about it together brings a great deal of solidarity to you as a couple, and a great deal of strength to your parenting arsenal as your child grows.

See also, "You Will Do Some Slightly Embarrassing Things as a Parent" (pg. 130).

[No.]
72

IT MIGHT FEEL AS IF YOU AND YOUR PARTNER LIVE

on SEPARATE PLANETS

Particularly if one of you goes back to work and one of you stays home, you and your partner may live wildly different lives for most of your waking hours—and this means you may find it both hard to relate to one another and difficult to empathize with the ups and downs of the other person's day. Add this to the already significant stress of becoming first-time parents and you have a powerful set of challenges facing your relationship.

First, there's the physical separation. If you've always been a couple who spends a lot of time together, the first day that one person leaves at 7 A.M. and doesn't return until nightfall can feel like an eternity for the primary caregiver. Chances are, you are not even able to chat on the phone or online like you might've before, much less sneak away for lunch or dinner after work. It can be a lonely feeling, for both of you—but probably mostly for the person spending twelve straight hours with someone who can't yet speak.

You may also—consciously or not—feel the urge to outdo each other, either out loud or in your head. "You think your *meeting* was stressful? Let me tell you what happened to me!" Each of you might be harboring some resentment, feeling jealous that the other person "gets" to go to work or "gets" to stay home with the baby. Each of you may be struggling to prove your worth, both to yourself and to each other. Each of you might be yearning for acknowledgment and validation on the job you're doing, while your partner doesn't even have a clear sense of what it is.

While second-time parents don't have any easy solutions to the relationship stress that comes with parenthood, they *have* learned to plan for it ahead of time. Follow their lead and, if finances allow, schedule a regular babysitter who will come one afternoon and/or evening a week, even for a couple of hours. This can allow for a movie or happy hour without breaking the bank. Look into co-op childcare, a babysitting share, or even booking your mother-in-law or a friend for a once-a-month date night. If you have friends with babies, talk to them about taking care of each other's infants one Saturday afternoon a week or something else that seems manageable. Or just make a pact that on Wednesday nights, after the baby is asleep, you order Thai food, open a good bottle of something, and talk to each other rather than folding laundry in front of the TV yet again. Catch each other up on your lives. Explain why the presentation was so important. Say why you felt frantic when you called about the baby's rash. Share your worries about how you're not doing a good enough job, or your uncertainty of what you want your future to look like. Talk, talk, talk. And don't forget to listen. Soon there will be less new-parent worry to grapple with and you'll be able to discuss other things too.

Second-time parents have had to learn to spread the love around as their family grows. By taking a cue from them and setting up couple time as part of the overall new family plan, you and your partner are not only ensuring some enjoyable time together, you are both acknowledging some important things: that you don't want to lose sight of each other, that you want to stay connected in crazy times as well as peaceful ones, and that the baby shouldn't be the only one in the family to enjoy your energy, affection, and attention.

See also, "You and Your Partner Will Argue—Possibly a Lot" (pg. 100).

[No.] 73 | YOU WILL SURVIVE TAKING
your **BABY** on the **PLANE**

Do you know who that howling baby bothers the most on the cross-country flight? The first-time mom or dad holding him. Really, everyone has endured the sound of a crying child on an airplane, and if it isn't your own, it's not so bad—headsets are common these days, plus the wailing gives all those people something to complain about until they hit ground again. Afterward, they'll promptly forget it. Meanwhile, you will likely sweat and stress through the whole flight and have the experience burned into your brain for months. Second-time parents are simply less worried about inconveniencing anyone—babies will do what babies will do, and crying on planes is one of those things. Here are a few tips to make it easier:

▶ **TRAVEL DURING NAPTIMES** when possible, or even bedtime for long trips. While you might get extra fussiness at the get-go, your baby might be tired enough to conk out.

SECOND-TIMER TIP

*Make sure your baby is wearing
a very fresh diaper before boarding. If you
must do a diaper change mid-flight,
remove as much of baby's clothing as possible
at your seat. Not all airplane bathrooms
have changing tables; if yours doesn't, you'll
have to maneuver a changing mat
over the toilet or sink.*

124
125

▸ **IF YOUR AIRPORT OFFERS A FAMILY LINE** at the security check-point, use it; if not, take the time you need and try not to stress about the people behind you.

▸ **NURSE OR BOTTLE-FEED** upon takeoff and landing, even if it's not time for a feeding (the sucking motion can help her ears adjust to pressure changes).

▸ **WEAR A SLING** or other comfortable baby carrier, helpful for both the airport and the plane.

*"Put two diapers on your infant for long
plane rides. The second diaper will absorb any
leaks and prevent you from having to dig
into your diaper bag when it's in the overhead
compartment and the seatbelt light is on."*
—MARISA, MOM OF 2, AGES 2 & EXPECTING

▸ **BRING A BAG OF GOODIES** baby has never seen before (especially helpful for older babies), like board books with lots of pictures.

▸ **BRING AN ENTIRE OUTFIT CHANGE**, pacifiers, and more food, formula, or diapers than you think you need. (Note that milk, formula, and baby foods are immune to airline rules for liquids and gels—but you must declare them at security.)

"For pee diapers on flights, I flip up the armrest, throw down a blanket or changing pad, and change the baby on the seat while kneeling in the aisle. It's much easier than the cramped bathroom."

—YUMI, MOM OF TWO, AGES 4 & 1

▸ **USE HAND SANITIZER** or antibacterial wipes to wipe down surfaces baby will be in contact with on the plane.

▸ **WALK UP AND DOWN** the aisle, over and over.

▸ **ASK FOR HELP**, again and again: board early, ask for a bulkhead row, and request boarding assistance if you need it. Talk to airline personnel about helping you manage all your carry-on gear. Talk to the friendliest flight attendant about switching to a row with more room. Ask a parent across the aisle to hold your baby while you dig in the bag for snacks. Whatever you think might help you, ask for it. Everyone wants your baby to be happy (meaning quiet), so they will likely be more than willing to assist you.

SECOND-TIMER TIP

If you're flying alone with your baby, most airlines will give your spouse or other family member an "escort pass" to accompany you through security to the gate, and to pick you up on your return. This is a lifesaver when you are carrying baby plus all your gear, and no one advertises it. Call your airline for details.

YOU CAN LET
your BABY CRY

We've mentioned this before, but it's worth saying again and again. This is one of the hardest but most essential parenting lessons: crying is not necessarily a bad thing. It does not equal failure on your part. It is your baby's only form of communication and his natural release from the stress of being a human being in a whole new world. The sooner you believe this, the better.

> *"With experience comes a very basic realization: most days, a crying baby is just as simple as being tired, being hungry, or needing a change. I remember with my first that I had created a fantasy list of at least ten things that could be wrong each time she cried."*
>
> —JANE, MOM OF THREE, AGES 10, 6 & 1

> *"Crying it out is really the only thing that will teach your baby to sleep through the night on their own. Don't wait until they're two and a half, when you'll have to come up with a creative, humane way to keep them in their room all night."*
>
> —TANYA, MOM OF TWO, AGES 3 & 2

YOUR BABY DOES
NOT NEED CLASSES

Two hundred bucks to send your baby to an education-minded music class for one hour per week? Forget about it. All children are inherently musical—they love simple instruments like drums, maracas, and tambourines; they love to wiggle to the beat; and they love most musical genres. There's no need for a teacher or even a *Mozart for Babies* CD. Invest in a couple of inexpensive instruments (rattles and pots with wooden spoons do just fine) and you'll be good to go.

If music is particularly important to you, play a lot of it in your house or car and sing to your baby. If you really want to go all out, make your own "music class" in your living room, and invite other new parents and babies to join you. Everyone brings an instrument or two (small baby-safe lidded containers filled halfway with dried beans or rice are perfect maracas) to toss in the middle of the floor for the kids, and everyone takes turns suggesting artists to listen to. Voilà! Your baby is enrolled in music class—one that is flexible and free.

The same goes for other types of courses that have become the rage for babies: baby signing, exercise, foreign languages, swimming. Signing her up at this tender age does not ensure a "head start" in these arenas, and forgoing them will not mean she'll somehow be disadvantaged. You have plenty of time to decide what classes might be the most enjoyable for both you and your child, and, in the meantime, just enjoy whatever interests you both each day. If you love the water, by all means take her to the pool; if you are a yoga nut, incorporate her into your poses at home; if you want to learn Italian yourself, play your tapes in the car— you don't have to take a class for any of this.

Of course, if you crave a scheduled activity, give a class a try, especially as your baby approaches one year or more. But if you don't, never fear— she can still make the high school swim team or master Spanish, even without attending a class in infancy.

See also, "You Don't Have to Subject Yourself to Kids' Music" (pg. 94) and "It's Okay for You and Your Baby to 'Do Nothing' All Day" (pg. 106).

[No.]
76

YOU WILL FIND YOUR OWN
PARENTAL COMFORT ZONE

So many questions will swirl around your mind before your baby is born, as well as during the first weeks and months. Besides the endless questions specifically geared toward your baby, there are many directed right back at yourself: *Should I travel with my infant? Go back to work or stay home? Use a nanny or a daycare center? Breast- or bottle-feed, and for how long? Keep my house neat or messy? Let my baby cry, and for how long?* All of these—and many more—can fit easily under one umbrella question: *What kind of parent will I be?*

"It felt like a kind of identity crisis to me," says one dad about the initial year with his firstborn. "Every choice felt like I was defining myself as a dad, and so I overthought everything. *Should I be the kind of dad who does this, or the kind who does that?* By the second baby, I could do a lot more by my gut."

Still, second-timers, by and large, continue to grapple with this question, because new scenarios never stop coming. And while they may not have all the answers, they do know one thing: you do come to find your own comfort zone as a parent, and it's as individual as you are. By the act of moving through each day with your baby, you will come to understand what is okay with you (perhaps ten minutes of crying is acceptable, but not thirty), what stresses you out (maybe restaurant meals but not airplane trips), and what you're particularly adept at and what you're not. You'll see that you have a totally different parenting style than a good friend or neighbor, and that you could never do it her way, even though her family is happy and fine. You'll slowly build up your own system of beliefs that work for you, and you'll discover books, doctors, and other parents with whom you agree and with whom you don't. You'll get comfortable saying, "That doesn't really work for us" about things that don't, with no excuses.

It's hard to know what your comfort zone will be until you're in the middle of it—and you might find yourself surprised. Also, if it turns out that you and your partner have different parenting comfort zones, you might have to work to find the intersection between them that is acceptable to you as a team. If Dad can't see what the big deal is about flying as a family to another coast, while Mom would rather stay home until the baby is in kindergarten, maybe you can agree on a short weekend jaunt—Mom can ease her fears and Dad can see the work involved in prepping for a trip. This is just one example in a long list of compromises two individuals must make when finding their way toward parenting as a team; ideally, negotiations are done with kindness and understanding of each other's particular style and comfort zone. When it gets tough to see eye to eye, remember that if you choose to have number two, some of this will be second nature (thank goodness).

[*No.*] 77 | YOU WILL DO SOME SLIGHTLY EMBARRASSING

THINGS *as a* PARENT

Here's an experiment. Check any of the following things you can't imagine doing:

▷ Making (and eating!) tuna casserole

▷ Wearing an old scrunchie or baseball hat to hide unwashed hair—for three days straight

▷ Staying in your bathrobe all day

- Owning more than one pair of clogs
- Crying every time you see a baby on TV
- Being unable to remember your last bath or shower
- Calling your spouse your child's name
- Thinking of an OB/GYN appointment or being stuck in traffic as your "alone time"
- Finding a solo trip to the grocery store luxurious
- Inventing not one, not two, but three different poopy songs to sing at diaper changes
- Pretending to be a trumpeting elephant in the middle of the mall to get your baby to stop crying
- Wearing your pajamas to the store
- Using your shirt as a baby wipe in a pinch
- Ditching date night after forty-five minutes because you miss your baby

If you've had more than one child, you know that you'll do all of these things—and, even more mortifying, numerous things just like them—*repeatedly*. Don't beat yourself up. You haven't given up, you haven't let yourself go, and you haven't turned into your parents. You are just in the very first throes of parenthood, and you are finding your way. Don't worry, you won't be in this stage forever—and until then, maybe you'll find out you can really rock a scrunchie.

YOUR BABY MIGHT WITHHOLD AFFECTION FROM THOSE

WHO CRAVE it MOST

Oh, the irony. Your mother has waited decades for her first grandchild, and every time she comes to visit, she gets nothing but ear-piercing wails. Or your sister has flown cross-country to meet her first nephew, only to be vomited upon repeatedly and treated with something akin to horror. Maybe even you or your spouse gets the cold shoulder. Meanwhile, a detached friend or stranger at the store gets coos and giggles. It's maddening.

This is a strange but common phenomenon, so you might as well be prepared for it. Know that particularly sensitive family members might be put off, or even angry, at your baby's lack of enthusiasm for their visits. Don't let it stress you out and don't take it personally. Second-timers have seen this happen before and know that it will pass . . . and that it's not anybody's fault.

While you really can't prepare or coax an infant to welcome or enjoy the person in question, you can do little things to help. Babies pick up on your own mood and tone of voice, so be conscious of greeting your visitors warmly and having time for everyone to acclimate together. If your baby seems skittish, holding him for a while will help assure him that everything's okay. Don't force interaction that he doesn't seem to want, no matter what your great-aunt says. But, after everyone gets used to each other, try to give your baby and the visitor some space—you might find that your baby is less frantic if you're out of the room and they have some time to get to know one another. You can also help by offering up best times of day, favorite ways of being held, a happy activity, and other encouraging tips.

In the end, everyone can do everything right and still find that they're getting no love. Your baby will come to know and trust other people when he is ready, and, like any individual, he will take to certain folks more than others for no discernable reason. The time will come, how-ever, when you will watch her run to hug Nana at long last, or play hide-and-seek with the uncle who used to never get a smile out of her. And from that moment forward, any ornery baby moments will be forgotten.

[No.] 79 | DON'T GET AHEAD of YOURSELF

When will she sit up? When will she talk? When will she walk? When will she sleep better? When will she stop fussing during diaper changes? When will she eat real food? It's easy to get wrapped up in what's lying ahead—and how that place might be better, easier, or more interesting. That's normal. We all skip ahead in parenting books to learn what our baby will be doing next, and we imagine how exciting that will be. New parents also tend to look ahead when it comes to far-off concerns, like how to potty train, what kindergarten to choose, and if the house will be big enough when and if a sibling comes. With all that forward-thinking, it can be hard to remember to relish the moment you're in. Try. Second-time parents realize that even though there are times that seem painfully slow, the first year really does go quickly. And as soon as she stands up on her own, that new baby will disappear before your eyes. Enjoy the slow moments you have before she starts running.

[No.]
80

LEARN HOW TO

BRING the PARTY to YOU

Your social life doesn't have to come to a screeching halt when you have a new baby. While it's great to go out on the town, the coordination, energy, and expense involved mean it probably doesn't happen as often as you might like. Skip the babysitter and do what second-time parents do—bring the party to you!

{

SECOND-TIMER TIP

Those baby-bottle brushes work beautifully for washing wine and martini glasses.

}

Blessed with sound sleepers, we've been having childless friends over for 8:30 take-out dinners, cocktails, or movie nights since our first child was a newborn. We find they are happy to oblige, and it keeps our friendships with them much more active than they would be otherwise, especially during that first year. Now that we have two kids, we've added a monthly open house into the mix when we throw our doors open for a block of time and invite friends both with and without children to come on over. What works best for us is midmorning, when one child is napping and one is full of good energy. We put out a pot of coffee, a bottle of Bailey's, and some store-bought pastries and get a chance to socialize with pals we haven't seen all month. The secret is making it easy enough that you will actually do it—and not worrying if your house is full of toys, laundry, and dust bunnies. Seriously, no one cares. What they care about is seeing you.

The same concept goes for having other new families over to your house. If you haven't already, you will likely make friends with other couples who have babies around the same age as yours—whether through a parents' group, birthing class, or just wandering around your neighborhood. If you wait for a day when you can make a meal that will work for both parents and babies, have your house cleaned up, and be certain your baby will be in the best possible state of mind, it will never happen. Now that we have our second child, we don't bother waiting for that kind of perfect alignment of the planets. Instead, we invite our friends and their children over—and ask them to pick up burgers on the way. We all gulp down our food, watch the kids play, try to cajole the older ones to consume something more than a french fry, and try to get the babies to swallow some yogurt—and along the way, we have some good (if disjointed) conversations and enjoy interacting with other people for a change. It's fun. No one worries about the mess, before or after the visit. Then the next time, we switch houses.

134
135

SECOND-TIMER TIP

Establish a recurring happy hour at your place to keep your social life active: just put out some self-serve mixed nuts, cheese, and wine, and ask pals to stop by on their way home from work or en route to dinner.

Remember, you *can* have people over—even if your house is a disaster or your baby's having a hard day, which will undoubtedly happen the first time you try one of these get-togethers at your place. Just offer up the invitation and let it roll. Let go, raise a glass, and enjoy the company of your friends—they have loved you since before the baby was born, and they still want to be around you, no matter what. It's up to you to let them. Cheers!

TRUST YOUR
INSTINCTS

Second-time parents don't read all the books—and it's probably not why you think. Even experienced parents don't remember everything from the various weeks or months of a baby's first year: what their baby should be doing when, what all the warning signs for various ailments might be, or what the best first finger foods are. But what they have learned, and remembered, is that their own unique child is *not* the child in the books. That means not all information and advice applies, no matter how much you read. Sometimes, you just have to trust your gut.

> *"After my first, I absolutely refused*
> *to read any serious baby or child-rearing books.*
> *I find I'm much less stressed!"*
>
> —JANE, MOM OF THREE, AGES 10, 6 & 1

"After purchasing and reading through a library's worth of baby books after my first son was born, I realized with my second to take all of those books with a grain of salt," says a mom of two. "If I don't no-cry-baby-whisper my kid to sleep or superfood him with complex porridges, he's still going to turn out just fine. And I won't feel like a failure when my baby doesn't react in all the ways the books say he should. Each child is a completely different person, and he's the one who's going to tell me best what he likes and needs, not a book."

This may be tough to swallow as a first-timer, when you are just starting to hear your inner parental voice. But give credence to that little voice and, over time, you will hear it more—and come to believe it more. If you just feel in your gut that your baby needs to be picked up (even though you decided to let him cry), that the rash needs to be looked at, or that the daycare isn't right for him—listen. If you don't agree with the advice in that parenting book that all your friends swear by, disregard it. If your pediatrician or childcare provider's recommendations seem at odds with your own sensibilities more often than not, find another one. You are the parent. And while you owe it to your child to be educated and aware of the many do's and don'ts for the first year of life, you also owe it to your child—and yourself—to trust your own instincts.

When you do use advisers, choose them wisely. There are so many books to choose from, not to mention a ridiculous amount of parenting advice on the Web. How do you avoid reading seven different books with, for example, seven different "sleep systems"? It can be as over-whelming, or more so, than shopping for all the baby stuff. You've got to limit your information to keep from going crazy. Have a small stable of credible sources, say, your pediatrician; a couple of trusted friends or siblings whose parenting techniques you admire; and maybe one book (recommended by one of these people) that speaks to you. Move beyond these when and if a particular issue warrants it, but not before.

[No.] 82 | **PEOPLE WILL CONSTANTLY COMPARE THEIR OWN BABY**

(FAVORABLY) to YOURS

Believe it or not, it happens from day one: everyone from your delivery nurse to your mother to the new dad at the park will ask you specific details about your baby—and then compare yours with their own. Here are some things you'll probably hear (repeatedly) during your first few months as a parent:

> *"How long was your labor? Well, that's not half as long as ours . . . "*

continues >

▸ "How old is he? Really? He looks so much bigger [or smaller] than that!"

▸ "You're lucky you don't have to deal with brushing hair— my baby was born with a full head of curls!"

▸ "My baby is sitting up [crawling, smiling, walking, eating solids] now! Is yours?"

▸ "Isn't it great that by this age, they're sleeping through the night?"

▸ "What percentile is your baby in? When my baby was that age, he was off the charts!"

This is a game you can't win, people. So resist the urge to try. Trust us, if your baby smiled today, theirs laughed; if yours was placed in the ninetieth percentile, theirs was in the ninety-fifth. It's nothing personal. Chalk it up to the fact that new parents have a deep-rooted need to share with one another, and, unfortunately, that need often is accompanied an urge to cast the most positive light on their own offspring, especially the first time around, when every milestone is so new and all-consuming.

> "Try not to sweat all those milestones and percentiles. The first time, you worry if your baby isn't doing everything right on schedule. The second time, you just shrug and say no, she's not sitting up yet. They all get there, and who cares who's first? I always like to say, 'Everything evens out by kindergarten.'"
>
> —ERIN, MOM OF TWO, AGES 8 & 4

"Don't try to raise the next Obama.
By the second child, you realize that maybe
your kid's gifted, but probably not.
Maybe your child will launch it three hundred
yards off the tee by the time he's eight, score
one hundred goals in his first year of hockey, or
read **Harry Potter** *when he's three, but*
it's doubtful. Just enjoy what you've created,
enrich his life, and try to stop comparing
your kid to the neighbor's."

—GORD, DAD OF TWO, AGES 10 & 7

It's kind of sweet when you think about it: these parents are truly in wonder of the being that they've created, and they want you to be in wonder
too. They are in the throes of new love and pride, wherein they only see
the good—and, in fact, they unconsciously exaggerate it. It's really
not about slighting your own baby. Rest assured, you may do it too. If
you haven't already, the day will come when you fudge a little about
how much your own child has grown or how many words he can say
(or someday, what he scored on the SATs). So until then, do what second-
timers do when faced with the comparison game: relax, smile, congratu-
late them on their little genius, and go home knowing, with every fiber of
your being, that you have the best, smartest, most beautiful baby in town.

[No.] 83 | YOU'VE GOT
to **EXPERIMENT**

Second-time parents have had a lot of time to learn that not
every child-rearing problem is solved by reading another book,
talking to another mom, or valiantly staying on course with
what you think should be the right method. Sometimes you've just
got to experiment, experiment, experiment. It's the only way to figure

out what's working right now, this minute, on this day of your baby's life—ever-changing and fluid and unique as it is.

If, for example, you're suddenly having trouble with your baby's morning nap, try putting her down a half hour later—or a half hour earlier. The results may surprise you. If the music she used to love no longer works during witching hour, try a brisk stroll—even if it's 10 P.M. If she's now refusing all green baby food, try heating it up—or serving it cold. If she's become more needy in the afternoon and you're frustrated with having to be at her beck and call, create spots in the house where she can make her own discoveries—low drawers and cupboards filled with board books or plastic containers, favorite toys hidden under the coffee table. If she's screaming every time you buckle her in the car seat, create a new song or game to go with it—or try just putting the car seat on the other side of the car to mix things up.

> *"When we decided our kids would share a room, it took two to three weeks of them getting used to each other, and then no sleep problems. So much for all the hours of worry I put in as to whether it would work, whether it was the right thing to do, and on and on."*
>
> —PAULA, MOM OF TWO, AGES 8 & 6

A cornerstone of successfully parenting a baby (and later, a toddler) is a willingness to find new tricks—and constantly evolve them. And there's only one way to do that: by throwing different things against the wall until something sticks. It's great to get ideas from other people who've been down a similar road, and by all means, try them all. But that isn't the end of the journey. What works in the books, or for your neighbor or your sister, may not work for you and your child today—and maybe not ever. The longer you're a parent, the clearer it becomes that the only way to discover your own personal bag of tricks that *work* for your baby is by trial and error. Put in the time to try everything you can think of, and go into it understanding that some things will work and some won't. What do you have to lose? Chances are you'll find an "aha" solution to whatever is plaguing you right now, and you'll emerge feeling victorious—and every inch the experienced parent you're becoming.

DON'T TRY
to BE a HERO

Many first-time parents want to show that they have it all under control. It seems to be a matter of (vigorously defended) pride. They do everything themselves, rarely leave their baby's side, and never let anyone see them sweat. They repeatedly say how great everything is, even at times when it isn't. They know no one can know or love their kids as well as they do—so they have a hard time letting go and releasing control to anyone, whether a highly skilled nanny or their own parents. After all, parenthood is the hardest and most important thing they've ever done—and they want to pass the test with flying colors.

Don't let yourself fall into what second-timers know is a very common trap. Parenthood shouldn't feel like a test you have to ace to be worthy; it is a process and you are *supposed* to be learning as you go. It's not only okay to need help, it's a good thing—it sets the tone for the rest of parenthood. Do you want to be the kind of mom who has to pretend she's holding it all together, when what she really needs is to shout "Help me!" from the rooftops? The kind of dad who feels like he's the only one in the universe who can comfort his child when he falls or take him out for some fun? The kind who can't admit when a break is desperately needed? We doubt it. But while second-timers are constantly admitting the cracks in their armor and trying to figure out how to find more healthy breaks from their children, first-timers are often saying, "Oh, I'll do it, I'll do it—he likes *me* to do it."

Remember, assistance is almost always available, if you are not too proud to ask for it. Believe it or not, those people who offer help actually *want* to help, so if you could just tell them you want it too, everyone would be happy. And they might even have a different way of doing things that your baby enjoys (and that you can learn from), if you are willing—so let friends or relatives take charge now and then. Raise your hand and tell your partner you need a night off. When it comes to paid help, that money spent on a house cleaner, cook, or babysitter might be worth its weight in gold when it comes to your mental health. Go ahead and use the money you might've spent on shoes, movies, or dinners out during your old life to hire somebody to vacuum, make a meal, change all the sheets in your house, or take your baby to the zoo. It's okay. You don't have to do it all. It doesn't mean you're failing if you need—or just want—a little help now and then, and say so loud and clear. Everyone knows you're a terrific parent, that's beside the point. Remember that old saying "It takes a village to raise a child"? Well, there's a reason it's an old saying. It's true. Let others help and you—and your baby—and everyone will be better for it.

See also, "Find a Support System—Early" (pg. 37) and "You Can Leave Your Baby with Other People" (pg. 98).

[*No.*]
85

GIVE YOUR BABY SOME ALONE TIME

with **EACH PARENT**

As much as family time is vital, it's also important to give your child dedicated time with each of you. There's just a different—and essential—dynamic that develops when you are one-on-one. No matter how totally compatible and comfortable you are with your partner, for example, you simply behave differently toward your baby when there is no other adult in sight. And you find new, unexpected solutions when you have no one but yourself to rely on in challenging moments. This is particularly important if one of you is the primary breadwinner and rarely gets solo parenting time.

The time you spend one-on-one doesn't have to be a big event or even a long period—just an hour or two of lying on the floor and playing can cement your individual bond with your baby *and* boost your confidence in your own parenting chops. Dad might discover a goofy bath-time game when left to his own devices with junior; Mom might invent a new favorite baby breakfast while Dad sleeps in. Not only will your baby be thrilled, you'll have another useful skill to add to your parenting tool-box—and you'll be proud of yourself.

[*No.*]
86

YOU WILL FEEL LIKE THERE'S NEVER ENOUGH
of YOU TO GO AROUND

"Most days, I feel nobody gets my best."

"When I'm at home, I feel distracted by work. When I'm at work, I'm wishing I were at home."

"I'm late for everything. My life is one mad dash from home to daycare to the office and back again."

"I don't give my baby, my partner, or my job 100 percent. I just can't. And I don't give myself *anything*."

Sound familiar? No matter how carefully you plan for your post-baby life, it is hard to prepare for how stretched you will feel. Stay-at-home parents, as well as those who work part- or full-time, all have difficulty juggling the myriad demands on their time and energy. Usually, along with that balancing act comes a nice heaping portion of guilt. Sometimes you may feel like you're failing absolutely everyone—a particularly tough feeling for those who have always felt quite in control or even tended toward perfectionism.

> *"With our second, we learned not to make any rash decisions about the future in the first three months. After our first baby, I was sure I wanted to stay home and almost quit my job. Six weeks later, I was ready to go back to work!"*
>
> —ELINOR, MOM OF THREE, AGES 10, 8 & 6

Experienced parents have come to learn that this stretched feeling may never entirely go away; it's as much a part of parenthood as the slobber marks on your favorite shirt and the clutter in your living room. Over time, you just get used to it: you wear the shirt anyway, and you step right over the debris without really seeing it. To survive, you have to let it recede into the background to some degree. When you fall into bed at night, instead of counting your shortcomings, think about the small victories, and rest assured that if you have a house in which kindness and love are prevalent, your child will be more than fine.

You, on the other hand? If the push-pull seems too overwhelming most days, talk to your partner and other parents. Sometimes venting about it—and hearing other people commiserate—can help a lot. So can quieting therapies like yoga, massage, meditation, and long walks, if you can find a way to work them in. See a therapist who specializes in parenting and family issues if that sounds right to you. Find one day—or even one afternoon—on the calendar each month that is your personal time, when you don't have to hurry anywhere and can be exactly where you want to be. This is what mental-health days are for.

If you feel you need a bigger change in order to feel more satisfied in this new role you're in, try writing down an ideal schedule and thinking about ways to get closer to it, whether that's talking to your boss about your hours, contemplating a career change or job share, or going back to work after a period away. If you're at home, think about bringing in or increasing childcare or housework help, and, if that's not feasible, start a babysitting swap with a friend or neighbor. Be patient; you may have to experiment a while before you figure out how much time you want to devote where. And, of course, this is always changing depending on decisions you make as a family about your finances, childcare choices, and careers. Understand that it can take a long time to settle into a balance that feels mostly right to you most days—but you will.

[No.]
87

YOUR OWN CHILDHOOD WILL COME INTO

PLAY as a PARENT

Somewhere inside you is a boatload of memories of your own early childhood and family dynamics. Many of these have probably been sitting there latent for years. Nothing like your first crack at parenthood to bring 'em all out.

Many second-time parents have learned this from experience with number one and have (hopefully) come to recognize some of the patterns they tend to fall into out of habit and family history. Perhaps Dad finds himself getting angry more easily than he'd like (a pattern from his own family) during year one with his firstborn. If he and his partner take the time to talk about the source of this as their child grows, and have consciously decided on ways to handle it so the legacy won't continue, then it will be less of an issue—not to mention less of a surprise—with baby number two. First-timers struggle with finding this kind of perspective, because they are so overwhelmed at just being a parent. There's simply not a lot of time for reflection.

The old saying about those who don't study history are doomed to repeat it holds true here. Whether it's a desire to distance yourself from or embrace your own upbringing, that family history does come into play, one way or another. Recognize this, talk with your partner about it, and you'll be more in control of what happens next. Think about the things you liked and didn't like about your own early childhood, your parents' parenting style, and the sibling dynamics in your family. What do you remember? How might this affect the way you parent? How will it influence your family?

Did your parents have very high expectations of you? Or in hindsight, do you think they were too lax? Were they not around enough, or overly protective? Were they temperamental, or even-keeled? How did your family show their love for one another? Considering all of this now—and continuing a dialogue about it—can help keep you from repeating patterns without being aware of where they're coming from. And as you think about these things, remember to also look hard at the good stuff— the rhyming notes your dad used to leave on the kitchen counter, the tradition of pancakes shaped like animals on Sundays, the way your mom always encouraged your interest in art; those will be legacies you want to be sure to carry forward.

[No.] 88 | YOUR BABY WILL BE AN INDIVIDUAL, AND NOT NECESSARILY

WHO you'd EXPECTED

Seems so obvious, doesn't it? But it's one of the hardest and most important parenting lessons you will likely wrestle with the first time around: your baby is not you. Your baby is also not the baby you had envisioned throughout your pregnancy. Your baby is his own person, with his own path. That means your child could very well have a different appearance, temperament, and personality than you could have ever imagined—and probably will, as part of the grand joke that parenthood sometimes seems to be.

Some of these differences will show themselves early, in babyhood (or even in the delivery room), and others will emerge later—but rest assured, they will come. It's helpful to remember in these moments that you can't expect your little bundle of joy to have only the adorable qualities of your family—your grandmother's eyes, your dad's laugh—without also some of the negatives.

> *"I'm not sure any of us teaches the first child great conflict-resolution skills, because we have the time to hover. I notice my third child, especially, handles her 'business' just fine, and I suspect it's because I didn't have the bandwidth to rush to her aid immediately."*
>
> —JODY, MOM OF THREE, AGES 8, 6 & 2

Sometimes their differentness will be a wonder, and, as with any new love, you will adore them even more for all the new things they open up to you. Other times, everything that makes them different from you will seem impossible to bear. With your first child, the temptation may be to nudge him to be something like what you had expected. You try to get your quiet child to love birthday parties and big family gatherings. Or like us, you try to get your high-energy baby to enjoy the quiet. And while it's certainly all well and good to encourage qualities that are important to you and your family, it is far more vital that you begin the long and important process of recognizing and accepting *who your child is*.

Certainly, your baby will evolve and change greatly with every passing week, month, year, and major milestone—just like any person. Take solace in the fact that a personality trait that you find distressing or difficult to relate to may soften, or not even hold. This journey is a roller coaster, people. Things you worried about last month will be forgotten, and things you never even considered will be on the horizon tomorrow. There is no sense in killing yourself trying to enact a personality change in your child any more than it's worth trying to change your spouse, and no sense in spending your time frustrated or disappointed by what he is not. Do your best to celebrate who he is right now, today, in this moment. Try to end each day talking about the good stuff.

By the second child, you realize that part of the wonder (and the immense challenge) of this endeavor is not knowing where it will lead, while embracing the potential of this developing person. Be as patient as you can, and open your eyes to who is growing in front of you, rather than picturing who you'd thought was going to appear. To quote from one of my daughter's favorite books, *Pinkalicious*, when you choose to become a parent, "You get what you get and you don't get upset." Words to live by.

| A LITTLE TV
WON'T HURT

We never had the TV on with our first baby. Seriously, *never*. We imagine our first child thought our flat-screen TV was a piece of big, black modern art. The only times she saw it on before the age of two were brief moments of playoff hockey as she was heading to bed (in fact, when she saw a TV in a book, she called it "hockey"). Our second child? Her first word may very well be "Ariel." She sees scenes from *The Little Mermaid* and *Cinderella* on a fairly regular basis—and is, not surprisingly, fascinated by all the color, music, and movement (plus the excitement of her sister). We literally have to pry her away from the DVD player.

> *"Everything is sacred the first time—*
> *naptime, babysitter selection, food selection,*
> *et cetera. I often wonder if this fostered*
> *our first's 'chosen-one' mentality. I am a strong*
> *believer in routine, but a little spontaneity*
> *and mess could help a firstborn learn*
> *to adapt more quickly."*
>
> —JODY, MOM OF THREE, AGES 8, 6 & 2

Do we purposely put our baby in front of the TV? No. But do we worry if she gets some secondhand TV exposure during the limited times when it's on? No. It just seems silly to deprive the whole family of our Saturday morning ritual of *Sesame Street* on the couch just because our baby is awake and might look at the screen now and then. So when you want to catch your favorite show or the last period of a big game, don't deprive yourself toooo much . . . just tell yourself that if your baby were a second (or third, or fourth) child, she'd be seeing a lot more of it.

[*No.*] 90 | # YOU CAN GO TO
CHILDFREE HOUSES

Afraid to go to brunch at a single friend's house because of the prevalence of breakables and lack of childproofing? Nervous to spend the weekend at your in-laws' because you picture every potential baby hazard in your mind, from power tools left on the porch to the jumpy family dog? It's natural to want to take your baby to only safe, protected, baby-friendly environments. But it's awfully limiting. With a tiny bit of advance planning, you can feel comfortable visiting your childless friends and family with your baby. (And hey, think of it this way: if a few things get broken, covered in spit-up, or peed on, it will be a good learning experience for everyone.) When second-timers know they'll be in a non-baby zone for a while, they do the following things without thinking twice:

- **CONSIDER PETS.** If there will be dogs or cats at home that are not amenable to babies, ask (in advance) that they be put outside or in a contained part of the house, and that any food bowls be out of baby's reach.

- **PUT AWAY REALLY FRAGILE THINGS.** Common sense, but if your baby is crawling or pulling up, delicate crystal vases and the like should be put out of reach. Give your host a hand as soon as you arrive so you can relax the rest of the time.

- **SWEEP FOR CHOKING HAZARDS.** Before letting your baby roam freely, check quickly for bowls of nuts on coffee tables, coins, decorative beads or pebbles, and cords. It only takes a few seconds to move things to higher ground.

- **KEEP AN EYE ON FOOD AND BEVERAGES.** Remember, childless folks will leave their cups and glasses on coffee tables without a thought—just like you used to. Drinks—especially hot coffee—should be kept away from baby's crawl zone, as should off-limits food.

- **BLOCK THE STAIRS.** A well-placed piece of furniture or even couch cushions can temporarily block stairs from a crawler.

- **CHECK THE OUTLETS.** Normally, you can keep a close enough eye on your baby to make sure he's not exploring any electrical sockets, but if this is a particular concern, throw a couple of socket covers in your diaper bag (or a piece of masking tape can do in a pinch).

If you plan to stay for several hours or overnight, you may want to consider bringing a carrier, a play yard, a portable high chair, or an infant seat so that you have a safe place to put baby for limited periods.

DISCIPLINE IS NOT
a FOUR-LETTER WORD

Your new baby is not out to get you (although it can feel like it sometimes). It's just that as your sweet little thing starts to explore the world, he will begin to realize the control he's slowly gaining over his environment—and that means he will start exacting that power, consciously or not. Every new parent will run into some advice on how to start influencing this new behavior, and that word—discipline—may rear its head. But before you reject the concept as a different way of saying "punishment," learn to embrace the word as it should apply to your baby: to discipline is to give him conscious, consistent teaching to help him learn about the world.

The Latin root of the word discipline is *discere*, and it means "to learn." The number one role of the parent is as teacher, and it starts from the very beginning. No, you won't be teaching your new baby the alphabet or the words to "Itsy-bitsy Spider" anytime soon, or even the difference between right and wrong. This isn't yet the time to consider time-outs or sticker charts to teach proper behavior. But you will quickly be teaching him important life skills, such as how to self-soothe, to avoid things that are hot or otherwise unsafe, to communicate and adapt to the world outside of your detailed ministrations, and much more. You will also start the endless process of teaching him day-to-day behavior, like not to repeatedly throw food from the high chair or pull the cat's tail.

A good example of discipline is when you decide to transition your baby into his own room. Regardless of the methods you've chosen, this is a learning opportunity for your baby. If you are having a difficult time with things like crying and separation anxiety, it's vital to remember that with each new experience, discomfort can be part of the process. It's true for babies, for children, and for adults—but through this discomfort and this learning experience, we grow. You and your partner will have to decide your limits over and over again, but remember that the ultimate goal is to *teach* your child a new life skill. And with everything you teach, you, as the parent, learn something too.

[No.]
92 | DON'T FREAK OUT IF YOU DON'T
LOSE the BABY WEIGHT

If you're like most couples, both of you might realize—when you actually have time to stop and look at yourselves—that parenthood has come with few extra pounds. It's normal. You have plenty of other things to worry about right now, so collapsing into tears when your pre-baby jeans don't fit is simply not worth it (even though you probably will shed some tears at some point). Yet, particularly for moms, the post-baby body can become a highly emotional issue.

Why does this particular weight gain seem so much more monumental than the eight pounds every American packs on over the holidays? It can be for a lot of personal reasons, including worry that your attractiveness has waned with parenthood, that you'll never get your old body back, or that you can't seem to manage accomplishing anything these days. Self-perception and self-worth can take a beating the first year of parenthood, when you are trying to find your way in an utterly new role, spending every ounce of energy on what is sometimes a thankless job, and questioning both your competence and every choice that led you to this place. The ill-fitting jeans can be the last straw. After all, if you were thin and toned, you would certainly feel like a million bucks, right? Those criminal "body after baby" pictures on the magazine covers don't help either, glorifying unrealistic Hollywood bodies that have bounced back at ridiculous speeds thanks to round-the-clock chefs, trainers, and nannies, while you are left standing in the grocery line with diapers and ice cream.

Cut yourself some slack. Second-timers know only too well that you are doing your first year's residency of the toughest job in the universe, and you are doing great. Your body has not failed you; in fact, with pregnancy and childbirth, it has succeeded at its single most amazing accomplishment and is still moving, bending, stretching, and lifting a thousand times a day. Start thanking your body for the work it's done, and try to be proud of it, lumps and all. You've come through the equivalent of ten marathons, and you are constantly performing a very physical job, even if your body doesn't seem to show it sometimes.

Of course, being healthy is important for your new life and all the energy it demands, so work on eating well and being active as your baby grows and becomes more settled. If a higher level of physical fitness is important to you, work with your doctor and your partner to create a reasonable regimen and goals—not so you can look like Jessica Alba in a bikini, but so you can feel well and strong.

[No.]
93

YOU WILL HAVE MIXED FEELINGS
ABOUT PARENTHOOD

Sure, every new parent has moments of feeling overwhelmed and stressed—and hopefully you'll learn to admit to those. But what about those deeper, more worrisome feelings, those little voices in your head that say, *Maybe this whole parenting thing is a mistake?*

Virtually every parent we talked to found the early weeks and months more challenging than they had ever imagined, and at times felt bewilderment, fear, anger, and a sense of being trapped. Many admitted, anonymously, that they were surprised to have second thoughts about the whole endeavor—but they did, and they were intense. One stay-at-home mom of a colicky baby felt the panic early. "I kept telling my husband the baby was broken," she admits. "I wanted to take him back."

For others, it came later, even during periods when everything was going fine on the surface. "There are moments of wonder," says a dad of a nine-month-old. "But there is also this feeling of 'what have I done?'"

There's no way to sugarcoat it: parenthood is tough. And you can't back out of it. Like any huge undertaking in life, it can be the hardest at the beginning, when everything is new and strange and not at all as you might have pictured it. If you planned and hoped and waited for this time to finally come, you might be surprised and ashamed at your ambivalence once you have the real thing. If pregnancy was more spontaneous, you might feel blindsided and unprepared. But, as opposed to other big undertakings, like a new job or a new city, it can be hard to admit—even to ourselves—that things aren't going the way we had imagined.

> *"At the end of the day, your firstborn will always be your firstborn, whether she is a baby or not. Each stage that Kat goes through is the first time my husband and I have experienced it from a parent's perspective. We remember that we are always crossing uncharted territory with each day that passes."*
> —JANE, MOM OF THREE, AGES 10, 6 & 1

Many first-time parents feel too guilty to say what they are really feeling: failure, regret, worry, incompetence, ambivalence. "I'm so lucky to have a healthy baby after lots of failed attempts to get pregnant," says another friend. "So shouldn't I be happy? Everyone expects me to be!" First-time parents dealing with these complex emotions often smile and say everything is terrific, then find themselves crying in the car on the way to the grocery store, yearning for a different life.

Your mixed feelings will come and go, but they will never go away. Sometimes you will feel an intense regret about how you could've lived your life differently if you were childless. Other times it will be a fleeting and bittersweet longing for the kind of fun you and your partner used to have before the baby was born. And then, as unexpectedly as they came, those feelings will disappear—for now—as you revel in your new family. Remember, it wouldn't be real life if you didn't question your choices, revisit the paths taken and not taken, and mourn a little for the life you used to have.

Take a cue from experienced parents and don't bury your feelings about this life-changing journey of parenthood—and how it has kicked your behind. Talk about it with your partner and with friends who are in the same boat. Choose a couple of experienced parents who give sound advice or are good listeners, and invite them over. Choose a professional to talk to if you feel you need it. Remember, rarely does anything meaningful in life work out exactly how we picture it will—but it does somehow all work out.

See also, "Go Ahead and Complain" (pg. 103) and "Find a Support System—Early" (pg. 36).

[No.] 94

HAVE FUN (AND TRY NOT TO BE TOO PARANOID) WHEN

INTRODUCING SOLID FOODS

"One of my second child's first solid foods was crisscross fries when he was seven months," admits one mom of two. "The lady at the next table looked shocked!"

First-time parents tend to be much more vigilant than second-timers about what goes into baby's mouth. All your other books—not to mention your doctor—spend a lot of time telling you what *not* to have for the first year. But what's *okay* for your baby to eat? What will she like?

Once your doctor signs off on your baby's readiness for solids (around six months), you will likely be advised to start with runny rice cereal, followed by strained fruits and vegetables, and then finger foods, avoiding things on the what-not-to-eat-until-one-year list. Luckily, pretty much anything is fair game to be a finger food as long as you cut it small enough and cook it until it's soft. In fact, many pediatricians think mashed-up versions of what you're eating will be tastier and more interesting for your baby than jarred baby food. Think about what you'd rather eat.

The typical advice is to start with single foods and wait for three or four days before introducing each new food to check for allergies, though most parents can't remember to strictly adhere to this. Then, as your baby moves into the nine-to-twelve-month stage, you can relax a little and really start to have fun with what you offer. After all, it's the beginning of a delicious, wonderful world of food!

Truth be told, second-time parents can't always take the time to prepare special "baby foods" for one member of the family, much less spoon-feed baby food at every meal. Their solution? As soon as possible, they give their babies small portions of the family meal, meaning if meatloaf, mashed potatoes, and green beans are on the menu, that's what baby eats too. And usually that's what baby *wants* to eat anyway.

"I remember doing an elaborate platter of chopped first-foods for our first baby, plus all that jarred baby food," recalls one mom. "It was so much prep. Our second would only tolerate baby food—or being fed by someone else—for the first couple of months of solids. After that she'd scream if she wasn't eating what we were eating. It worked much better to just mash up our meals and let her pick them up herself. Suddenly, I could eat too!"

Of course, second children also get tastes of things their parents never authorized—candy, snack crackers—thanks to those helpful older siblings who "share" with them in the backseat of the car. And who knows, maybe all of this makes them more adventuresome eaters later in life.

SECOND-TIMER TIP

Resist the urge to buy a padded, cushy high chair—it only offers more nooks and crannies for sticky food to hide in. Babies are already wearing cushy little diapers and are just fine sitting in hard molded-plastic high chairs, which are much easier to hose down over and over again.

To that point, don't as a rule avoid strong flavors or spice; do you think babies in other cultures get stuck with applesauce and rice cereal? Once you have the okay from your pediatrician that your baby is physically ready to experiment, let her taste your pad thai with tofu, bean-and-cheese burrito, chicken curry, or chili with cornbread. If she's reaching desperately for your onion rings, let her try a bite. Of course, you should avoid obvious allergens, especially if you have a family history of food allergies. But the point is, use common sense and let her explore. She'll let you know if she likes it or not. Encourage the unbridled excitement she likely has right now for all kinds of food—after all, she'll be surviving solely on mac-and-cheese and crustless jam sandwiches before you know it.

> *"A little chocolate won't kill 'em!*
> *My in-laws laughed when they saw my one-year-*
> *old son eating chocolate at Halloween—*
> *they reminded us that our daughter didn't get*
> *a chocolate bar until she was three!"*
>
> —LYNE, MOM OF TWO, AGES 4 & 1

[No.] 95 | THE FINANCIAL STRESS OF PARENTHOOD can be GREAT

If you were to ask any experienced parents about the financial costs of raising a child, you might expect them to give you a number. More likely, they'll smile, shrug their shoulders, and say, "Oh, a lot." There is no question that the majority of new parents underestimate what a child can potentially cost. Now, many people will argue that raising a child is not about the cost, it's about the love, and the family . . . and we agree. But to ignore that element of starting a family is not only questionable but can be disastrous.

> **SECOND-TIMER TIP**
>
> *Once you can pinpoint where the costs lie,*
> *you'll discover the simple savings strategies of*
> *experienced parents, like consignment stores,*
> *babysitting swaps, and free activities.*

Depending on which experts you talk to, the cost of raising a child to adulthood can be staggering. Regardless of where your child ends up falling on the cost spectrum, you are the ones paying the bills—so it makes sense to be as prepared as you can be. Find a financial planner. Decide what's important and what's not, both in how you spend money on yourselves as parents and in what you expect to spend on your child. Talk to each other to make sure you are on the same page when it comes to spending: Are family vacations paramount? Is private school a necessity? Are you both okay with secondhand furniture in order to put money elsewhere?

"With my first daughter, I felt the need to buy her the best of the best. I wasn't going to have some pre-spit-upon play mat for my kid. So I shelled out massive amounts of dough for transient pieces of brand-new baby gear that got, on average, three to four months' usage, max—and took up way too much room to save for number two and beyond. With my second, we borrowed or bought used versions of whatever we could—bassinet, swing, stroller, high chair—because we knew we'd only use them for a short time and then pass them on.

—JENNA, MOM OF TWO, AGES 5 & 3

While you don't have to make any firm decisions now, and your views will no doubt evolve as you go, putting some thought into this now may help stave off surprises later. ("You spent *how much* on that?") And, to the best of your ability, put away money for a rainy (college) day and let compound interest do its magic.

As your child grows, you will be exposed to the various expenses (discretionary and not) that come with a baby; be mindful of how little things can add up. It's easy to get caught up in spending on that first child—of course, you want him to have the best of everything. But the earlier you start saving the money that could have gone for the sixth cute sweater in the same approximate size, the more you're relieving the financial stresses of the future. And, as if you needed another benefit, it's a strong lesson in how to handle money that your future allowance-earner will learn from.

[No.] 96

YOU'RE ALLOWED TO SKIP HOLIDAYS OR A

big FIRST-BIRTHDAY PARTY

Our first baby was born in August, and when people cooed at her and said, "What are you going to be for Halloween?" we learned to say, with a smile, "Eight weeks old!" Were we really supposed to wrestle a costume onto a newborn? It was the same story for Christmas, when family members expected to see a picture of her with Santa—in a special outfit for the occasion, of course. We found ourselves having to justify our lack of motivation to take a new baby to stand in line with crowds downtown and be plopped onto a strange man's lap. By her first birthday, though, we did follow convention—a small but traditional birthday party with guests, goody bags, decorations, and a cake. That was fun, and something we truly wanted to do.

First-time parents seem to think these kinds of year-round milestones are expected of them, though, and that they might be somehow failing their kids or disappointing the grandparents if they don't comply. Second-time parents? They're too tired or busy to worry about it, much less make excuses for it. They do the things that matter to them, or their children, and skip the rest. You are allowed to do the same—even the first time around. "I started planning my first child's birthday party months in advance," says a friend. "For my second, it was whittled down to what I felt was the essence of a birthday: a present, a candle, a sweet thing to eat. We sang the song and took the photos, and we wore party hats

because that was important to my older daughter. It was just our immediate family, and I remember it just as well, if not better . . . with none of
the stress attached to the memory."

LET GO OF THE IDEA OF A CLUTTER-FREE HOME

Let's face it: babies come with a disproportionate amount of stuff from the get-go, all of which threatens to overtake your house on a daily basis. Stumbling over it all the time is not only an exercise in frustration, on difficult days it can feel like a mudslide sweeping your previously peaceful and tidy life away. Second-time parents fall into three categories when it comes to dealing with this reality:

1 *Those who have totally succumbed to their house being taken over by children's stuff*

2 *Those who continually try to weed out, clean up, and maintain some semblance of order*

3 *Those whose homes show no evidence of children whatsoever*

We're pretty sure that the number ones are the most content, the number twos are most common (yet likely the most aggravated), and the number threes are, well, creepy.

You've undoubtedly already seen how much clutter comes with parenthood from the moment your baby shower ends. If you are one of those people who likes everything in its place, it can be disheartening to see your home now jammed with a bassinet, crib, rocker, changing table, infant seat, carrier, swing, jumper, stroller, play mat . . . not to mention all the clothes, toys, and supplies. Will there ever come a day when you're not tripping over the giant box of diapers or stubbing your toe on the safety gate? Well, yes. But by then you'll be tripping over the trike and stubbing your toe on the dress-up box. There's always *stuff*, and like it or not, as the kids get bigger, sometimes their stuff does too.

Experienced parents' advice? Let go a little. It's up to you how much— but it's important that you and your partner come to an agreement so that you feel you're working together to keep your environment the way you want it. You do not have to let your entire house become an unedited baby zone, but you also do not have to battle to make it look perfect— because both of these options will likely cause you undue stress that you simply don't need.

> *"Kids only know what you show them.*
> *I have a good friend whose son's room was a*
> *walk-in closet until he was five years old.*
> *It worked beautifully for everyone."*
> —ELIZABETH, MOM OF TWO, AGES 1 & 1

Make some basic bottom-line decisions about what's important. You may decide, for example, that outgrown baby gear will go into storage or to charity immediately, and that all toys will be off the floor and tossed into bins before baby's bedtime. That's doable, and once your baby is sitting up, you can have her "help" you put her things away as part of her nightly routine. Or you might find you need to do this twice—once at a naptime, so you're more able to relax, and once again at bedtime. That's okay too. If you're lucky enough to have an extra room or a large closet, you might decide that all portable baby items live there and are only brought into the other living areas as needed. The key is not falling into the trap of repeatedly performing the same clean-up a dozen times a day, which will only make you feel like you're pushing the proverbial rock up the mountain but never getting to the top. And don't fall into the other trap, the one where you feel like a failure if your house is a mess. Kids *should* come with a little mess.

"My neighbor has two children, one tiny box of toys in the living room, and no clutter whatsoever—even when I stop by unannounced, there's not even books on the table or shoes piled by the door," a friend says. "You can't even tell she has kids. But I'm not even jealous. It's too weird!"

[*No.*] 98 | IT CAN BE EASY
BEING "GREEN"

Over the past generation, the concept of "green living" has shot to the front page. And rightly so. It's no wonder that this topic now frequently pops up when talking about the raising of a child, and what that child does to your family's carbon footprint. Which is better, cloth or disposable diapers? Are plastic toys made in China okay? Is your formula organic? Are you going to raise a vegetarian or a vegan? If you want a bigger car, should it be a hybrid? Being a first-time parent is stressful enough without having to worry that the mere presence of your new baby is throwing the world into environmental chaos. Luckily, there are simple things you can put in place to help make your new family green— and second-time parents, who struggled through those decisions with their first child, have learned not only how to implement them but how they can make life easier and more economical.

If being environmentally conscious is important to you, create an informal "green plan" that outlines the steps you can take to gently incorporate your newest member into your family's carbon footprint. Seek out the advice of other like-minded parents on how they are approaching this. Most of all, remember that every effort, no matter how small, is worth it—and take pride in knowing that you are trying to better the world in which your child will grow. On the next page are some thoughts:

DIAPERS. Yes, disposables wreak havoc on the environment. But surprisingly, so does cloth. There are many studies that support either side, pitting landfill versus water consumption and cleaning chemicals. No matter how you slice it, your baby will be using a lot of them, and they are hard on Earth. Think about working to offset this by reducing your own personal waste output and choosing the greenest version of whatever type of diaper or diaper company you select. You may also want to investigate new chlorine-free, biodegradable, or flushable diaper options.

WATER USAGE. Some estimates place the baby-related increase of water consumption near the one-hundred-gallon-a-day mark. Ouch. Try washing the baby's laundry with yours, use a thermos to keep water warm throughout the day instead of running the tap, and remember that daily baths are not necessary for your little one—and note that all these environmentally friendly habits are time-savers for you too.

ELECTRICITY. Think about how many electronic products are associated with a baby, and you can see that meter spinning. Consider using LED lights, a nice soft lighting choice for a nursery. Don't overdo the heaters or air conditioning, as not only can these be costly for you, they can irritate small lungs. Find alternative ways to engage your baby other than with plugged-in toys and contraptions. Still concerned? Many urban areas now have an option to purchase "green" energy; if it's in your budget, consider using it as an offset.

▶ **FOOD.** When it's time for solids, invest in a great set of small sealable containers to avoid throwing out food (and money). Second-time parents know that babies often need several attempts at a food before it's accepted, and consumption often fluctuates greatly. Also look into your community's green-waste programs or get a tabletop compost bin and enrich your garden.

▶ **PRODUCTS IN GENERAL.** Ask questions about ecofriendly products and look online to find those that use fewer chemicals and less energy. Buying fewer clothes and gear for your baby and using your local consignment store (or swapping with other parents) is a great lesson in reduce-reuse-recycle, which goes a long way to saving both the environment and your pocketbook.

[No.] 99 LIKE IT OR NOT, YOUR BABY WILL COME TO ADORE

LICENSED CHARACTERS

Here's the reality: by the time he's one year old, your baby may come to deeply love Winnie the Pooh or Tinkerbell—even if you do nothing to encourage it. In fact, this mysterious connection will happen even if you tightly restrict his exposure to TV and his access to anything other than handcrafted toys and classic board books. It's kind of inexplicable how it happens, but it does happen. Ask any second-time parent. Try as you may to stave off the onslaught of Dora and Disney characters until at least toddlerhood, somehow they begin to infiltrate in babyhood. When you become a parent, you suddenly see that licensed characters are everywhere—they're on your newborn's diapers, every sippy cup in sight, and myriad grocery store items, from soup to macaroni. Don't be surprised when your baby excitedly reaches out for a box of Hello Kitty crackers long before he can say "Mama."

Needless to say, these familiar faces have been thoroughly researched and designed to elicit a positive response from even babies. And it's okay to give in to whatever reasonable licensed character seems to bring your child great joy, even if you can't understand or appreciate why. After all, throughout his life there will be plenty of things that he finds irresistible and you find annoying, hideous, politically incorrect, or all of the above. Second babies are indoctrinated into this world even earlier (our number two could accurately point out every Disney Princess by name in her older sister's books, even before she could speak), thanks to their older siblings usually being around preschool age, the prime time for this sort of thing. As long as you aren't strongly opposed to whatever your baby has attached to (say, a Bratz doll in a micro-mini), just let it go. It doesn't mean you're endorsing a huge commercial empire to let him have SpongeBob SquarePants shoes as his first birthday present. It just means you're a parent, and a door has now opened that leads to the toy store—and to the passionate whims of a child discovering what's colorful, friendly, familiar, and placed at eye level at every turn.

[No.] 100

IT'S OKAY TO THINK LONG AND HARD ABOUT

HAVING ANOTHER ONE

Enough said. But just think of how much easier it's going to be the next time around!

E

F

G

H

ACKNOWLEDGMENTS

The authors would like to sincerely thank their friends and families, and all the fellow parents from coast to coast who offered up their (extremely valuable) spare time to contribute insights and enthusiasm to the book. We couldn't have done it without them—and we learned a lot, too.

We would also like to thank our two daughters, the inspiration for this book and so many other endeavors, and the wonderful community of friends that they've brought into our family's life.